# LOST RIVER TOWNS *of* BOONE COUNTY

# LOST RIVER TOWNS *of* BOONE COUNTY

EDITED BY BRIDGET B. STRIKER
FOREWORD BY DONALD E. CLARE JR.
CONTRIBUTIONS BY JENNIFER GREGORY, C. ADAM HARKE, MELINDA SARTWELL & LAURIE WILCOX

THE History PRESS

Published by The History Press
Charleston, SC 29403
www.historypress.net



First published 2010

Manufactured in the United States

ISBN 978.1.59629.472.1

Library of Congress Cataloging-in-Publication Data

Striker, Bridget.
Lost river towns of Boone County / Bridget Striker.
p. cm.
Includes bibliographical references.
ISBN 978-1-59629-472-1
1. Boone County (Ky.)--History, Local. 2. Cities and towns--Kentucky--Boone County--History. 3. Historic sites--Kentucky--Boone County. 4. River life--Kentucky--Boone County--History. I. Title.
F457.B65S26 2010
976.9'363--dc22
2010024443

# Contents

Loading passengers at Petersburg for the trip to the Fernbank Dam celebration, September 4, 1911. Fernbank Dam was located near Taylorsport in northern Boone County. *Courtesy of the Petersburg Album Collection, Boone County Public Library.*

# Foreword

It is always such a thrill to rediscover something that has been lost in time. It's an even bigger thrill when that thing is a town, especially a Boone County, Kentucky town along the Ohio River.

The entire northern and western boundary of Boone County is the Ohio River, 35 beautiful miles of it. For the past twelve thousand years, human beings have been traveling the waters of this 981-mile Ohio River, and for twelve thousand years, they have passed what is now Boone County, Kentucky.

The Paleo-Indians, the name given to the very first Native American culture to inhabit Boone County, began their nomadic lives of following their main food source, the megafauna of the Pleistocene era, in North America about 10,000 BC. The mammoths and mastodons followed their food and water sources down the glaciated midsection of the continent, leading the Paleo-Indians through Boone County and along the Ohio River, the natural corridor most conducive to travel. And these early inhabitants made stops along the way and lived for periods of time along the river. Not quite in towns per se, but these were the embryonic beginnings of specific sections of settlement by human beings.

Man and animal continued to travel this very same route in search of subsistence and sustenance throughout the next cultural period, that of the Archaic Indian. Still mainly hunters, these early inhabitants were also gatherers, utilizing plants, nuts, fruits and grasses to complement their diet. The Archaics were not quite as nomadic as their predecessors, and they had seasonal camps and temporary settlements along the river. There were subsections of the Archaic, called Early, Middle and Late Archaic Periods, covering a span of about six thousand years. Archaic Indians of each of these periods spent time here in Boone County, living for periods on the banks of the river. The settlements were still not quite towns but were getting closer.

The next Native American cultural affiliation—the Woodland period Indians, also subclassified into Early, Middle and Late—dates between the years 1000 BC and AD 1000. It was within this period that the use of pottery appeared. Later in the period, earthworks and burial mounds began to dot the Boone County landscape. Again, there is archaeological evidence of seasonal camps and temporary gathering spots, but no large permanent village sites.

It was during the last period—the Late Prehistoric period—that we find evidence of more permanent settlements and a change toward a sedentary and agrarian lifestyle. This is also called the Fort Ancient period. It is represented by village sites along the river and creeks that are of a more permanent makeup, indicating continuous habitation. Petersburg sits atop two of these Fort Ancient villages, one dating in the vicinity of AD 1250–1400 and the other, AD 1450–1600. There are many other similarly documented Fort Ancient village sites within the county borders.

It wasn't very many years beyond this that European contact occurred. Again, those who explored and traveled the New World did so either by river or on foot following the rivers and smaller tributaries. As the Europeans continued down the Ohio River, two things occurred. First, diseases of the Old World were spread among the new continent's native inhabitants, in essence almost completely decimating their cultural propagation. The natives had no immunities against the European diseases because they had never before been exposed to cultures other than their own. Second, the North American continent became the object of desire of every major European power and was explored, claimed, traded, sold, taken and bartered back and forth, until finally it became its own free and independent country with a brand-new form of democratic government.

There were no ruling kings or queens, no officially established religion, no preestablished social castes. There were equal opportunity and rights for everyone. Soon, established settlement patterns surfaced, and they naturally followed the major waterways of our interior. In Boone County, the settlement patterns were easily identified and followed: down and along the Ohio River and up the major creeks.

The choice areas of settlement became the areas of most fertile soil and higher elevation out of the flood plains along the river and up the major tributaries of Elijah's Creek, Sand Run, Taylor's, Garrison's, Second, Woolper, Middle Creek, Lick Creek, Gunpowder, Landing (Little

Gunpowder) and Big Bone Creek. As people became subject to recurrent fevers and shaking chills (called ague), which they attributed to miasmas (harmful disease-carrying vapors from the bottomlands, which were in fact probably mosquito-borne conditions), they continued to follow the creek tributaries inland and upland for health reasons.

Before Kentucky became a state, it was a county of Virginia, called Kentucke County. It was customary at the time to reward and compensate members of the military with grants of land for their service. The amount of land granted was directly proportional to a soldier's rank, duration and quality of service. It wasn't unusual for a ranking general to receive a one- to two-thousand-acre grant of land here in Boone County. Old family names such as Piatt, Brown, Marshall, Ryle, Stephens and others began to settle here with military grants like these. As these families came to settle on their allotted land, some areas became hamlets and towns, and other settlements faded away into obscurity.

There was a U.S. military fort established and built at the mouth of the Great Miami River as it enters the Ohio River in Indiana across from Boone County. This was in the North Bend area, so named for the abrupt Ohio River course change there. Fort Finney was completed but never utilized or occupied because it was built in a major flood plain and was constantly inundated by the flood-prone Ohio. On the Kentucky side, across from Fort Finney, a settlement called Touseytown—formed in anticipation of a garrisoned fort's presence for protection from marauding Indians—was established at Second Creek. The other adjacent creek (Garrison Creek) was obviously named because of the establishment of Fort Finney, which was subsequently abandoned and rebuilt farther down the Ohio River toward Louisville.

Petersburg, being built on the very same site as two former Fort Ancient villages, began in 1788 as Tanner's Station, located directly across the river from the mouth of Tanners Creek as it enters the Ohio River on the Indiana side. The site for this town is high enough to have never been ravaged by any of the Ohio River floods, including the 1937 flood. Petersburg remains an extant, vibrant river town today. Touseytown is a mostly forgotten memory, preserved only in written Boone County history. This scenario repeats itself many times along Boone County's Ohio River shoreline. Grant survives in present times as Belleview Bottoms. Maxville (Mackville, McVille) survives only because of the former U.S. Government Dam #38. Meeks Landing at the mouth of Middle Creek is all but forgotten, while Rabbit Hash (formerly Carlton) remains the county's most celebrated and vibrant nineteenth-century river town. Managed by the nonprofit 501-c-3 Rabbit Hash Historical Society, it is one of only two National Register Districts and Preserve America Communities in Boone

County. Once a very large rural farming community, featuring Kirtley Landing and the Piatt's Winfield Cottage, East Bend now remains extant in name, with two churches, one active and the other inactive for half a century.

Farther downriver, the towns of Normansville and Hamilton Landing have survived in name and memory only. Big Bone Creek represents the boundary of Boone and Gallatin Counties but most significantly meanders through the North American continent's "Home of American Vertebrate Paleontology," Big Bone Lick, the most celebrated national and international Pleistocene megafauna fossil site known to science. Already designated by the Department of Interior as a National Natural Landmark, Big Bone Lick State Park is in the process of receiving National Landmark status, which will rank it in national historical and cultural significance along with Mount Rushmore and the Statue of Liberty. Remnants of the town of Big Bone remain today, most notably Big Bone Gardens and the Big Bone State Park.

Come explore and experience more of the history of the lost river towns of Boone County, Kentucky, as the Boone County Public Library continues its commitment and dedication to the preservation of our county's oral and written history and heritage.

Don Clare

This early twentieth-century postcard shows a group posing on Split Rock, located at the mouth of Woolper Creek, just south of Petersburg. It was common practice to take a pleasure boat out to the rock and spend the day exploring the area. *Courtesy of Don Prout, www.cincinnativiews.net.*

# Acknowledgements

The Boone County Public Library would like to thank the following people for their assistance: Thomas Schiffer, Don Clare, Bernie Spencer of www.nkyviews.com, Don Prout of www.cincinnativiews.net, Emmett Witham, Yvonne Edwards, Jeanette Edwards Smith, Melissa Humphrey, Tony Popp, Steve Borthoff, JoAnn McMullen Suttles and Alice Ryle. We would also like to thank our editor, Will McKay, for his patience and guidance throughout this process.

This 1883 *Atlas of Boone, Kenton and Campbell Counties* map shows the Boone County precincts and the location of the active ferries. This book follows the river from the northeastern end at Constance, through North Bend in the Bullittsville precinct, down the river past Petersburg into East Bend (Carlton precinct) and then south to Hamilton, covering over forty miles. *Courtesy of the Boone County GIS Database, Boone County Public Library.*

# Introduction

As Don Clare so aptly presented in the foreword, Boone County's long and rich history is directly tied to the flow of the Ohio River. From prehistoric times through the conflicts of European settlement and into the peaceful agrarian rhythms of the nineteenth and twentieth centuries, Ohio River travel has played an essential role in the daily life of the county.

After Kentucky became a state in 1792, migration steadily increased until Boone County was officially established, in 1799, with a population of fifteen hundred. Boone County's population continued to grow throughout the first half of the nineteenth century. Many settlers who came to the county were drawn to the fertile river bottomlands, establishing farms and towns along the river. The communities located along the Ohio River especially prospered during this time period. Interior roads were often nothing more than muddy, bumpy trails, making the river the most efficient and economical way to transport goods and people at that time. Riverboat landings lined the shore of the Ohio River, enabling residents of these riverfront communities to sell their surplus goods, as well as purchase essentials from traveling merchants.

The river communities of Boone County represent a larger migratory trend in the United States during this time period. Rivers were the most viable commercial arteries in the country, and towns were platted all along the Ohio River Valley. However, the Ohio River was not an optimal mode of travel. The deep river that we are accustomed to today is the result of damming in the twentieth century. Prior to damming, seasonal fluctuations caused the river to vary from deep streams to shallow pools, making it impossible for boats to pass at certain times of the year. With the arrival of railroads and improved interior roads, like the Covington–Lexington Turnpike, major transportation arteries shifted away from the river. With this change, the river communities began to fade away.

Boone County remained an agrarian society until the mid-twentieth century, when the transportation arteries shifted once again. The opening of the Greater Cincinnati/Northern Kentucky International Airport in 1947 and the construction of Interstates 71/75 through the county during the 1960s brought a rapid increase in population and development, making Boone County one of the fastest-growing areas in the United States. The concentration of development around the airport and the interstates has left those areas largely unrecognizable to longtime residents, while the river corridor has remained virtually untouched. With the construction of bridges between Kentucky and Indiana in the 1970s, the traditional ferries could not compete with the faster methods of travel. The focus away from the river has proved costly for the region, where many towns have been replaced with gravel pits.

Rabbit Hash has proved to be the exception to the rule as far as Boone County river towns are concerned. The jewel of Boone County preservation efforts, Rabbit Hash gained some national notoriety with its canine mayor and the general store that has been in operation since 1831. Rabbit Hash is a viable community with a solid tourist base and a strong sense of place. The Rabbit Hash Historical Society works tirelessly to promote and protect Boone County's river town history. For that reason, Rabbit Hash is not included in this book. Rabbit Hash is, quite simply, not lost.

We hope the reader will take this opportunity for a nostalgic look at vanished communities, silenced riverboats and empty fields—a way of life that has been swept away in the current of the Ohio River.

# 1
# Constance and Taylorsport

## Constance

German immigrants who settled Constance in the early nineteenth century named the town after Konstanz, a Rhine River town. Located at the mouth of Dry Creek, Constance grew up along the riverbanks around a popular ferry landing. The Mitchellsville–Dry Creek Turnpike (now Route 20) was the community's connection to the interior of the county. Constance stretched between the turnpike and the ferry landing, with tollhouses at the turnpike and Point Pleasant Road. The opening of a post office in 1853 signaled a period of rapid growth. Before the end of the century, Constance was a thriving community, home to a school, church and a variety of businesses. Familiar names long associated with Constance include Hempfling, Masters and Peeno.

A common theme in Ohio River towns is repeated flooding. In particular, the 1937 flood forced the evacuation of the riverfront. Residents had to abandon their homes and live in the community's school for a short time. The decline in population during the twentieth century prompted the closing of the post office in 1997, and the community is now home to the largest interstate water-transfer system in the United States.

A view of Anderson Ferry and the Kentucky shoreline taken from the Ohio side of the river. Notice the hillside advertisements for passing steamboats, much like highway billboards today. *Courtesy of Bernie Spencer, www.nkyviews.com.*

A view of the Constance school taken from the Mitchellsville–Dry Creek Turnpike (now Route 20). The turnpike stretched across the county from Constance to the Burlington–Petersburg Turnpike, making it a vital link between the western and northeastern sides of the county. *Courtesy of Bernie Spencer, www.nkyviews.com.*

A linear town that grew up around the Anderson Ferry, Constance spread out along River Road (now Route 8) and developed into a thriving little community that included wagon makers, grocers and blacksmiths. *Courtesy of Bernie Spencer, www.nkyviews.com.*

A store along River Road in Constance, circa 1900. *Courtesy of Bernie Spencer, www.nkyviews.com.*

A common sight along the turnpikes, this tollhouse was one of two located at Constance. Tolls were collected to help pay for maintenance of major roads. *Courtesy of Bernie Spencer, www.nkyviews.com.*

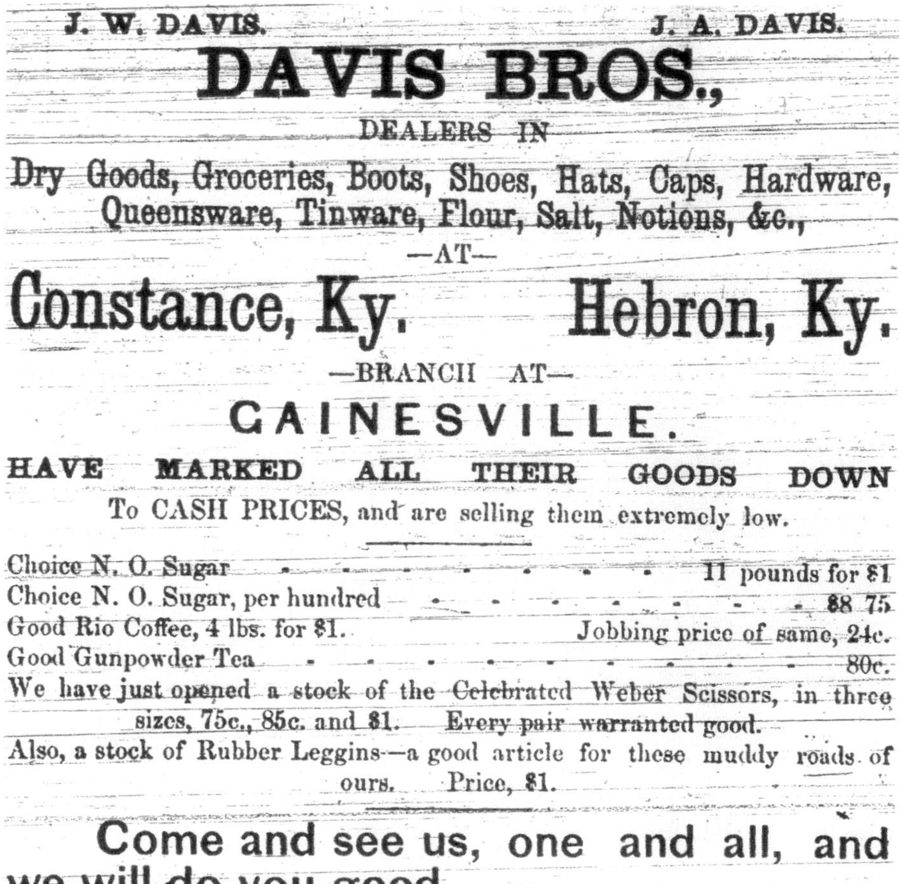


An 1876 advertisement from the *Boone County Recorder* for the Davis Bros. store in Constance shows the type of goods carried by general stores that were common in most communities. *Courtesy of Boone County Public Library*.

Benjamin F. Zimmer's store in Constance, circa 1900. The son of German immigrants, Benjamin married Louisa in 1874, and over the years they had at least eleven children. Benjamin ran the store in Constance, across the road from Anderson Ferry, for at least thirty years. *Courtesy of Bernie Spencer, www.nkyviews.com.*

A view along Route 8 looking east from Constance to Taylorsport. Stringtown is a tiny community that lies on the Ohio River between the two towns. *Courtesy of Bernie Spencer, www.nkyviews.com.*

# ANDERSON FERRY

Located in Constance, the Anderson Ferry is named for George Anderson, who bought it in 1817 from Raleigh Colston. The Andersons built a large stone house overlooking the ferry where the family resided and operated a tavern. The Anderson family owned the ferry operation until 1841, when son Evan transferred the property to Montague McClure. According to legend, the transfer was the result of a lost poker game.

The business changed hands numerous times until 1865, when Charles Kottmyer bought it for $2,800, along with two acres of land. Two years later, Mr. Kottmyer converted the ferry operation from horse power to steam power. Kottmyer's first steam ferry was christened Boone No. 1 in honor of Daniel Boone. Since 1857, nine ferries have been named for Daniel Boone, the last being Boone No. 9 in 1992. Four generations of the Kottmyer family owned the business until it was sold to Paul Anderson in 1986. It isn't certain if Paul is related to the original Anderson family. Today, three ferryboats make numerous trips across the Ohio River 364 days a year. It remains one of the oldest continuously running ferry operations in the United States, with over 190 years of service.

The Anderson Ferry stone house in Constance overlooked the ferry landing. Ferry owner George Anderson built the house in 1820 as a residence and tavern. The building stood on the property until the early 1970s. *Courtesy of the Fitzgerald Collection, Boone County Public Library.*

The Kottmyer/Hempfling family in front of the original Anderson Ferry House, circa 1907. Forty-two family members, ranging in age from infancy to over seventy-two years old, appear in the photograph. *Courtesy of Yvonne Edwards.*

The Anderson Ferry prepares to make one of its many daily journeys across the river to Anderson Ferry in Cincinnati, Ohio, circa 1950. *Courtesy of the Fitzgerald Collection, Boone County Public Library.*

A postcard view of the Anderson Ferry stuck in ice during the winter of 1918. Before the Locks and Dams System, the river level fluctuated dramatically between flooding and a water level low enough for a person to wade across. These fluctuations made the river impassable for riverboats. The extreme freeze of 1918 paralyzed river traffic and sank several steamers at the Cincinnati landing. *Courtesy of Bernie Spencer, www.nkyviews.com.*

## TAYLORSPORT

West of Constance on River Road is the small community of Taylorsport, located at the mouth of Elijah Creek. The community grew up around a warehouse and ferry established by Thomas Foulkes in 1827. General James Taylor, one of the largest landowners in neighboring Campbell County, developed Taylor's Ferry in 1836. By 1846, General Taylor had laid out a town called Taylorsville. The name of the town was later changed to Taylorsport. Unlike nearby Constance, the community has streets laid out in a grid pattern. Taylorsport had its own post office, which closed by 1959, a Methodist Episcopal church and a school. Families such as Canady, Crosby, Fox and Walton were prominent in Taylorsport in the 1880s.

The community fielded its own baseball team, which was a member of the Boone County League. Baseball was a popular pastime in the county from the 1870s until World War II. Nearby Parlor Grove brought many travelers through Taylorsport en route to the popular attraction. Jim Reis notes that in 1884 "ferry traffic between Cincinnati and Taylorsport was at an all-time high."

Even before the Ohio River Locks and Dams System was built in the twentieth century, Taylorsport had begun to fade away. The Locks and Dams System raised the water level of nearby Elijah Creek, taking out the entire west end of town. Little is left of the original town.

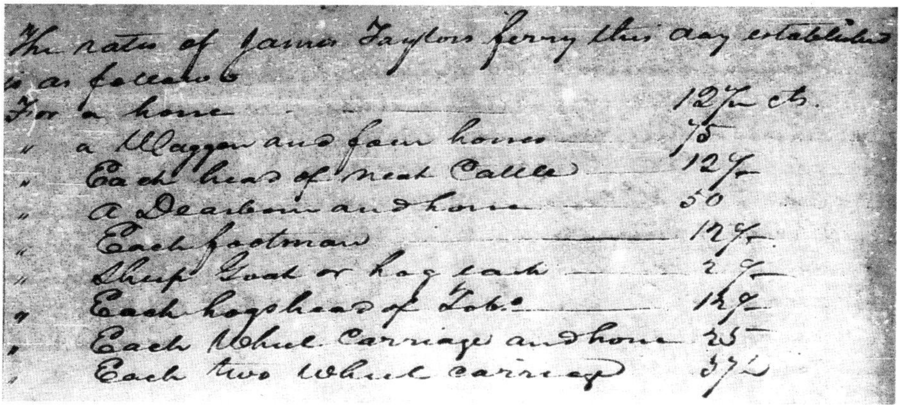

The rates of James Taylors ferry this day established is as follows
For a horse — 12½ cts.
" a Waggon and four horses — 75
" Each head of neat Cattle — 12½
" a Dearborn and horse — 50
" Each footman — 12½
" Sheep Goat or hog each — 2½
" Each hogshead of Tob.o — 12½
" Each One Wheel Carriage and horse — 25
" Each two Wheel carriage — 37½

General James Taylor, one of the largest landowners in neighboring Campbell County, established a ferry at the mouth of Elijah Creek in 1836. The court established ferry rates to ensure that ferry owners were charging fair amounts. General Taylor laid out a town around the ferry landing, initially called Taylorsville but later changed to present-day Taylorsport. *Boone County Court Orders 1836–1848. Courtesy of Boone County Public Library.*

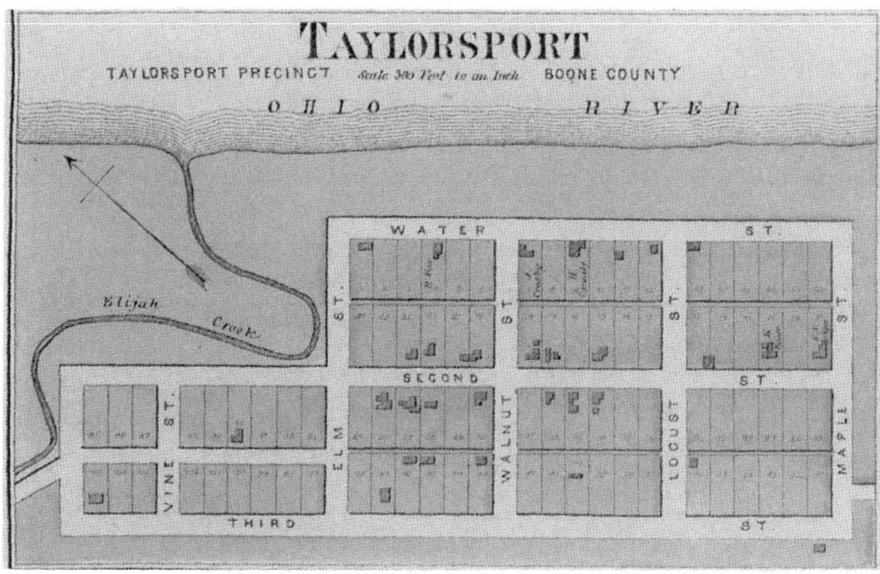


In 1883, D.J. Lake & Company published an atlas for Boone, Kenton and Campbell Counties, detailing property owners, county roads, waterways and towns. This view of Taylorsport shows the grid pattern layout and the town's proximity to the Ohio riverbank and Elijah Creek on the west end. *Courtesy of Boone County Public Library.*

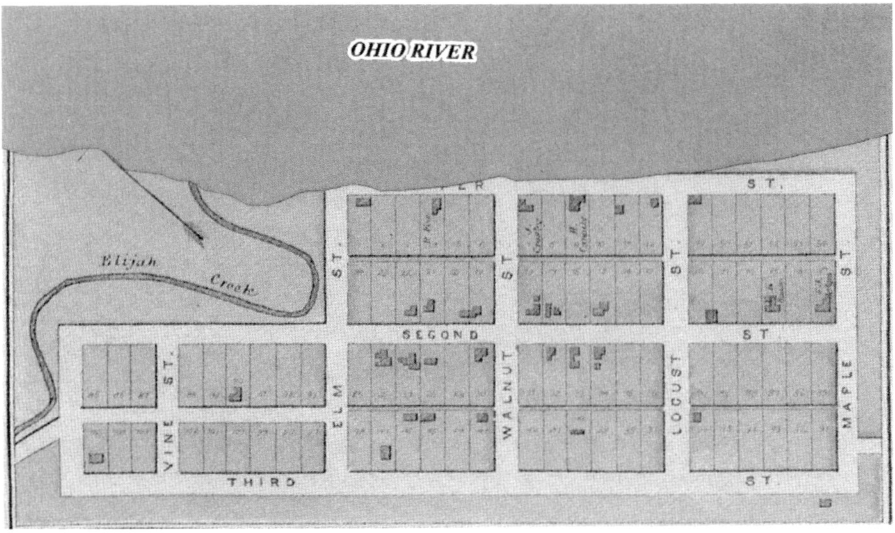


The same *1883 Atlas of Boone, Kenton and Campbell Counties* view of Taylorsport with a present-day GIS overlay shows the Ohio River now covering Water Street. Locust Street is also gone, as is the entire west end of town past Elm Street. *Courtesy of Boone County Public Library.*

The 1922 Taylorsport baseball team. *Front row, left to right*: Joe Hogan, Floyd Dill, Doc Goodridge, Jack Sprague, Ralph Sprague, Earl Morehead and Howard Acra. *Back row, left to right*: Hazel Walton, Tommy Goodridge, Ed Sanford, Harley Sprague, Terrell Sprague and Ben Zimmer. *Courtesy of Melissa Humphrey.*

Talyorsport residents Martin Aylor Jr. and Georgia Humphrey, daughter of Lewis and Ruth Humphrey, standing by the frozen Ohio River in 1948. The Aylor and Humphrey families were neighbors in Constance in 1920. *Courtesy of Melissa Humphrey.*

Georgia, Ruth Gladys (née Phelps) and Clyde Humphrey stand on the Elijah Creek Bridge at Taylorsport in 1925. Tragically, Ruth died from complications of tuberculosis in May 1928. *Courtesy of Melissa Humphrey.*

John Grim (standing in boat) and friends out for a day of fun on the Ohio River. Photograph taken near Taylorsport in 1914. *Courtesy of Melissa Humphrey.*

Taylorsport schoolchildren, circa 1930. *Courtesy of Melissa Humphrey.*

Virgil (left) and Clyde Humphrey, sons of Lewis and Ruth Humphrey, go fishing at Taylorsport, circa 1930. In 1920, Lewis was listed as a lock man at the Fernbank Lock and Dam 37. *Courtesy of Melissa Humphrey.*

Pericles "Boy" Grubbs stands on the turnpike in this early twentieth-century postcard. A grandson of local physician Dr. James T. Grubbs, Pericles spent his entire life farming in Taylorsport alongside other well-known farmers such as the McGlasson and Hempfling families. *Courtesy of Melissa Humphrey.*

*Above*: This 1950s panoramic view from the hill above Route 8 shows the farmland on the eastern side of Taylorsport and the Ohio River. *Courtesy of Melissa Humphrey.*

*Left*: Essie, Sadie and Edgar Earl Morehead take time away from play to pose for the camera in this circa 1910 photograph. Earl and his wife, Elizabeth, later owned the Morehead Boat Harbor near Taylorsport for many years, until it was destroyed by a tornado in 1974. *Courtesy of Melissa Humphrey.*

## Parlor Grove

Managed by the Reinhart brothers, Parlor Grove was located east of Taylorsport on the shore side of River Road. Used as a picnic ground as early as 1860, the park grew into a popular destination for day-trippers throughout the region. People would arrive by steamboat to spend the day playing games, listening to live music, dancing, watching sporting events and enjoying rides like the Flying Dutchman. Parlor Grove was also a well-liked spot for events such as community festivals.

By the 1890s, the Coney Island amusement park had opened east of Cincinnati, ending Parlor Grove's popularity. The Coney Island Company purchased the property before the turn of the century and then sold it in 1901 to farmer Charles O. Hempfling. Hempfling developed the site into an operating farm, selling a variety of produce to the Cincinnati-area markets. His son Liston continued to farm the Parlor Grove acreage, while his other son, Charles L., moved a mile or so downstream to found Valley Orchards in 1914. Valley Orchards was a popular roadside market, selling produce in a "U-Pick" setting.

In 2004, the Hempfling family sold seventy acres. They donated an additional eighteen and a half acres to Boone County, which will use the land as a sports complex. Recently, the fifth generation of Hempflings opened Valley Orchards Farm and Greenhouse, once again providing fresh produce, herbs and flowers to the community.

The *Thomas Sherlock* docks at Parlor Grove in this nineteenth-century lithograph. Parlor Grove was located east of Taylorsport and was used as a picnic area and amusement park as early as 1860. Boats brought passengers from Cincinnati and surrounding areas to spend the day enjoying music, sporting events, games and food. By the 1890s, its popularity began to fade with the rise of Coney Island, east of Cincinnati. The park closed at the turn of the century. The land was sold in 1901 to the Hempfling family. *Courtesy of Bernie Spencer, www.nkyviews.com.*

The Hempfling/McGlasson family. *Left to right, front to back*: Lilly Kottmyer Hempfling, Dorothy Conner Hempfling holding Anita Hempfling, Alice Quigly McGlasson, Lillie Conner, Hubert Conner, Charles O. Hempfling, Vaughn Hempfling, William T. McGlasson, Lizzie Mae Hempfling and Liston Hempfling. Charles Hempfling purchased Parlor Grove from Coney Island in 1901. *Courtesy of Yvonne Edwards.*

Walter, Charlie and Liston Hempfling standing in front of their wagon at Parlor Grove, circa 1913. The wagon seems to be carrying a young calf. Liston took over the Parlor Grove farm from his father, Charles O. Hempfling. *Courtesy of Yvonne Edwards.*

Liston Hempfling at the Northern Kentucky Apple Show in Covington on November 20 and 21, 1929. Liston was known for his award-winning apples, as was evident from his four ribbons and two trophies that year. *Courtesy of Yvonne Edwards.*

## Fernbank Dam (Lock and Dam No. 37)

Before the advent of railroads, settlers were almost entirely dependent on the waterways for commercial trade. The Ohio River was a major artery of interstate commerce. However, in dry weather the water was often so low that a person could walk across the river in spots, making river traffic impossible. The Army Corps of Engineers developed a system consisting of forty-nine locks and dams stretching from Pittsburgh to the Mississippi River. The Locks and Dams System allowed water levels to be adjusted along the length of the Ohio River, making year-round river traffic possible.

Lock and Dam No. 37, or Fernbank Dam, spanned the section of river between Taylorsport, Kentucky, and the village of Fernbank, Ohio. Construction began in 1905 and was completed, with much fanfare, the week of September 4, 1911. Steamboats crowded with passengers made the trip to see the new dam and celebrate its completion.

The Ohio River's Locks and Dams System had become obsolete by the 1940s. The bigger towboats that were being designed made it necessary to create a new dam system. The new streamlined system included only nineteen dams and could raise the water level to twenty-five feet, a dramatic increase from the nine feet of the previous system. As part of the new construction, the older Locks and Dams System was dismantled over time. The Fernbank Dam was closed and demolished in 1963. The property was part of the Hempfling sale to Boone County in 2004. There is nothing of the original dam structure visible today.

Fernbank Dam (Lock and Dam No. 37) was built in 1911 to help control the river levels. Located near Taylorsport, Fernbank was in operation until the 1960s, when it was replaced by the modern Markland Dam in Gallatin County, Kentucky. *Courtesy of Don Prout, www.cincinnativiews.net.*

Steamboats returning to Petersburg from the christening of Fernbank Dam near Cincinnati, September 5, 1911. According to the *Boone County Recorder*, the steamboats were participating in a parade as part of the grand opening celebrations for the new dam. *Courtesy of the Petersburg Album Collection, Boone County Public Library.*

Another view of the parade of steamboats returning from Fernbank Dam on Tuesday, September 5, 1911. The steamboat parade and christening were part of the weeklong grand opening festivities, which concluded with automobile races and "aeroplane" flights on Saturday. *Courtesy of the Petersburg Album Collection, Boone County Public Library.*

# 2
# North Bend

In 1773, Captain Thomas Bullitt came to the wilderness of the Ohio Valley to conduct surveys for land grants received for service in the French and Indian War. While in the region, Bullitt laid out what became Louisville, Kentucky. He picked out North Bend, Boone County, for his own claim before he left the area. Unfortunately, Bullitt died during service in the Revolutionary War, in either 1778 or 1782, before he could settle his claim.

In 1783, George Washington and a group of Continental and French army officers created the Society of the Cincinnati. According to the society's website, the purpose of the organization was to "preserve the rights and liberties for which they had fought and to foster the bonds of friendship that had been formed among them during the long years of war." Just upstream from Boone County, Losantiville was renamed Cincinnati in honor of the organization.

The region became a stronghold for society members, who settled on prime real estate all along the Ohio River. Colonel John Cleves Symmes of New Jersey was a founding member of the organization and was responsible for distributing lands to society members throughout the Ohio River Valley. Cleves, Ohio, and Symmes Township, Ohio, still carry the name of the New Jersey colonel. Cornelius Sedam, a New Jersey captain, settled what became Sedamsville, Ohio, just west of Cincinnati. Zebulon Pike, another New Jersey captain, settled in Lawrenceburg, Indiana. Future U.S. president William Henry Harrison, son of Virginia politician and signer of the Declaration of Independence Benjamin Harrison, had a farm in what is now North Bend, Ohio. The farm property was located right next to land belonging to Harrison's father-in-law, John Cleves Symmes. Today, members of the Symmes and Harrison families are buried in North Bend, Ohio, at Congress Green Cemetery, including President William Henry Harrison himself.

## CAVE JOHNSON

Cave Johnson (1760–1850) was a young adventurer, coming to Kentucky from Virginia in 1779 to help establish Bryant's Station, near the North Elkhorn River. For several years, Johnson traveled between Virginia and Kentucky. According to Johnson's reminiscences, in 1784 he married Betsy Craig, sister of John Hawkins Craig, and settled on Green Creek near Versailles. John Hawkins Craig served at Bryant's Station under Cave Johnson's brother, Captain Robert Johnson, in 1782 and was present during General Clark's Big Miami Campaign against the Shawnee. Craig was also the cofounder of Craig's Camp, now Burlington, Kentucky.

Settling in what was then Woodford County by 1789, Johnson was appointed clerk to the county and quarter sessions. In 1792, Craig signed over to Johnson and his heirs three hundred acres along the north bend of the Ohio River. Johnson moved to the property in 1796 and built a grand Federal-style mansion facing the river. The property was located along Sand Run Creek, across the river from William Henry Harrison. Cave Johnson frequently traveled across the river to visit Harrison.

Cave Johnson was commissioned a colonel of the Kentucky Militia about 1798 and held that post until 1811. He was active in politics and held many offices throughout his long life, serving as the first county clerk, as justice of the peace, as sheriff and as a representative in the Kentucky legislature in 1817. Johnson was a devout Baptist and is buried at the cemetery of Sand Run Baptist Church, a church he helped establish in 1819.

A postcard view of the Ohio River and the farmland along the Kentucky shore in North Bend. *Courtesy of Don Prout, www.cincinnativiews.net.*

A postcard view of North Bend, Kentucky, from North Bend, Ohio, near President William Henry Harrison's tomb. Colonel Cave Johnson's farm was directly across the river from the Harrison farm, making it convenient for the two men to visit. *Courtesy of Don Prout, www.cincinnativiews.net.*

*Above*: Colonel Cave Johnson's Federal-style house in North Bend. Colonel Johnson owned a large plantation, served as Boone County's first county clerk and as a surveyor. This circa 1797 mansion has been restored and is currently a private residence. *Courtesy of the Historic Structures Collection, Boone County Public Library.*

*Left*: The headstone of Colonel Cave Johnson at the Sand Run Baptist Church cemetery in North Bend. Colonel Johnson is buried beside his family directly behind the church. *Photograph by Melinda Sartwell.*

## Sugar Grove Plantation

Around the bend west of Colonel Johnson's land lay another large plantation owned by Captain John Brown (1752–1824), who also served in the American Revolution. Captain Brown was from New Jersey and moved to North Bend during the 1790s after purchasing 650 acres from the Christopher Clark land grant. Brown also frequently crossed the Ohio River, visiting his close friend Colonel John Cleves Symmes. Nothing is known about Brown's wife; Captain Brown lived on the large plantation with his only surviving child, Clara Harlowe Brown, born in 1783.

In March 1801, young Lieutenant Zebulon Montgomery Pike (1779–1813) married Clara in Boone County. Pike was the son of Zebulon Pike of Lawrenceburg and Isabella Brown, reportedly John Brown's sister. While Clara stayed behind at Sugar Grove, Pike was assigned to various frontier posts. In 1806, he led an expedition to explore the Southwest, discovering the mountain known as Pike's Peak. By 1813, Pike had risen to the rank of general and was sent to Sackett's Harbor on Lake Ontario for a campaign against the British. He was killed by flying debris during the Battle of York and buried at Sackett's Harbor, leaving Clara a widow with young children. The only Pike child to reach adulthood was a daughter, Clarissa Brown Pike, who married John Cleves Symmes Harrison, son of President William Henry Harrison, in 1819. Tragically, John died in 1830, and Clarissa died in 1837, leaving behind six children whom Clara raised at Sugar Grove until her death in 1847.

The original Sugar Grove mansion is said to have burned down sometime in the 1840s, taking much of Zebulon Montgomery Pike's memorabilia in the fire. The home was later rebuilt farther inland, using the bricks from the original mansion. In the early twentieth century, the Southgate family became the owners but never lived on the property. Over the years, the mansion became uninhabitable and eventually burned down in the 1980s. Located beyond the end of the county-maintained Route 8, the property bears no resemblance to the majestic plantation it once was. The cemetery is the only reminder of the Brown/Pike/Harrison story.

Portrait of General Zebulon Montgomery Pike. *Courtesy of the Library of Congress Prints and Photographs Division, Washington, D.C.*

View of the Pike/Brown/Harrison cemetery in North Bend, circa 1950. Located on what is now private property at the west end of River Road (Route 8) on the grounds of Captain John Brown's old Sugar Grove Plantation, the cemetery is overgrown and mostly forgotten. *Courtesy of the Fitzgerald Collection, Boone County Public Library.*

The headstone of John Cleves Symmes Harrison in the Pike/Brown/Harrison cemetery in North Bend. Harrison, the son of President William Henry and Anna Symmes Harrison, married Clarissa Pike, daughter of General Zebulon and Clarissa Brown Pike. *Courtesy of the Fitzgerald Collection, Boone County Public Library.*

# BULLITTSBURG

In 1797, Cave Johnson requested permission from the Campbell County Court to plat a hundred-acre town named Bullitt's Bottoms, or Bullittsburg. Bullittsburg is mentioned in Campbell County court records at various times—there is even a reference to a specific lot in the town—but a search of the court books in Campbell and Boone Counties has not revealed a plat map. According to a descendant of Cave Johnson, it is believed to have been platted near the western corner of Johnson's property, directly across from North Bend, Ohio.

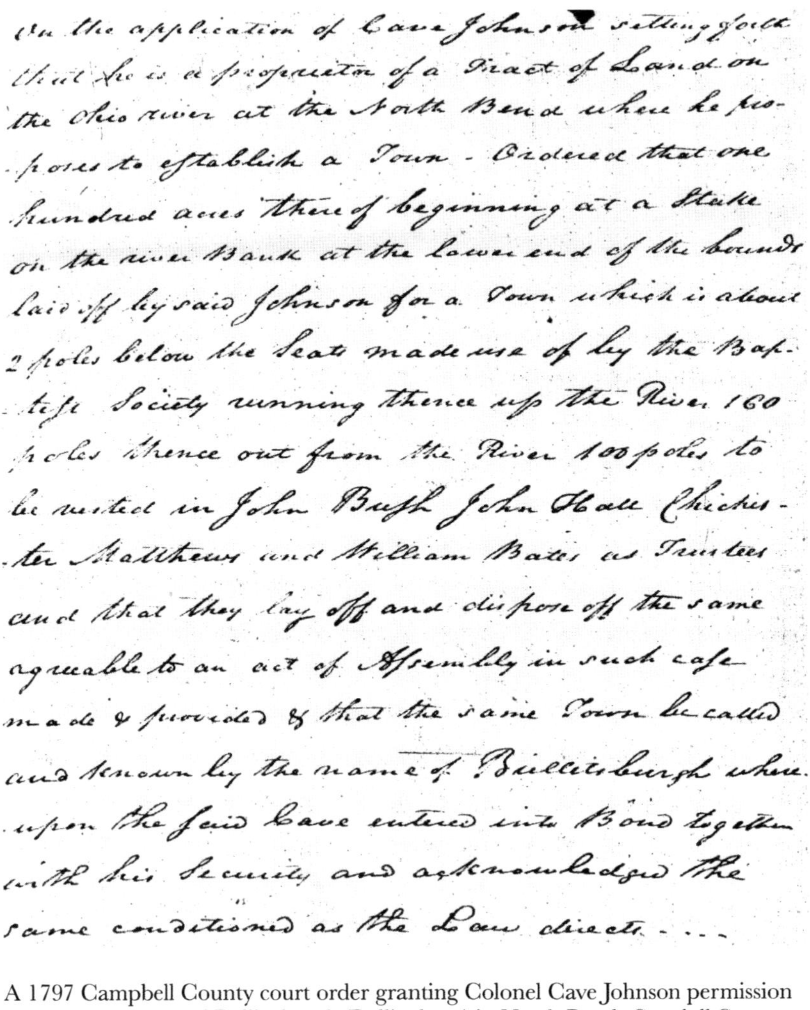
On the application of Cave Johnson setting forth
that he is a proprietor of a Tract of Land on
the Ohio river at the North Bend where he pro-
poses to establish a Town - Ordered that one
hundred acres thereof beginning at a Stake
on the river Bank at the lower end of the bounds
laid off by said Johnson for a Town which is about
2 poles below the Seats made use of by the Bap-
tist Society running thence up the River 160
poles thence out from the River 100 poles to
be vested in John Bush John Hall Chiches-
ter Matthews and William Bates as Trustees
and that they lay off and dispose off the same
agreeable to an act of Assembly in such case
made & provided & that the same Town be called
and known by the name of Bullitsburgh where-
upon the said Cave entered into Bond together
with his Security and acknowledged the
same conditioned as the Law directs. . . .

A 1797 Campbell County court order granting Colonel Cave Johnson permission to plat a town named Bullittsburgh (Bullittsburg) in North Bend. *Campbell County Court Orders Book A. Courtesy of the Campbell County Clerk, Alexandria, Kentucky.*

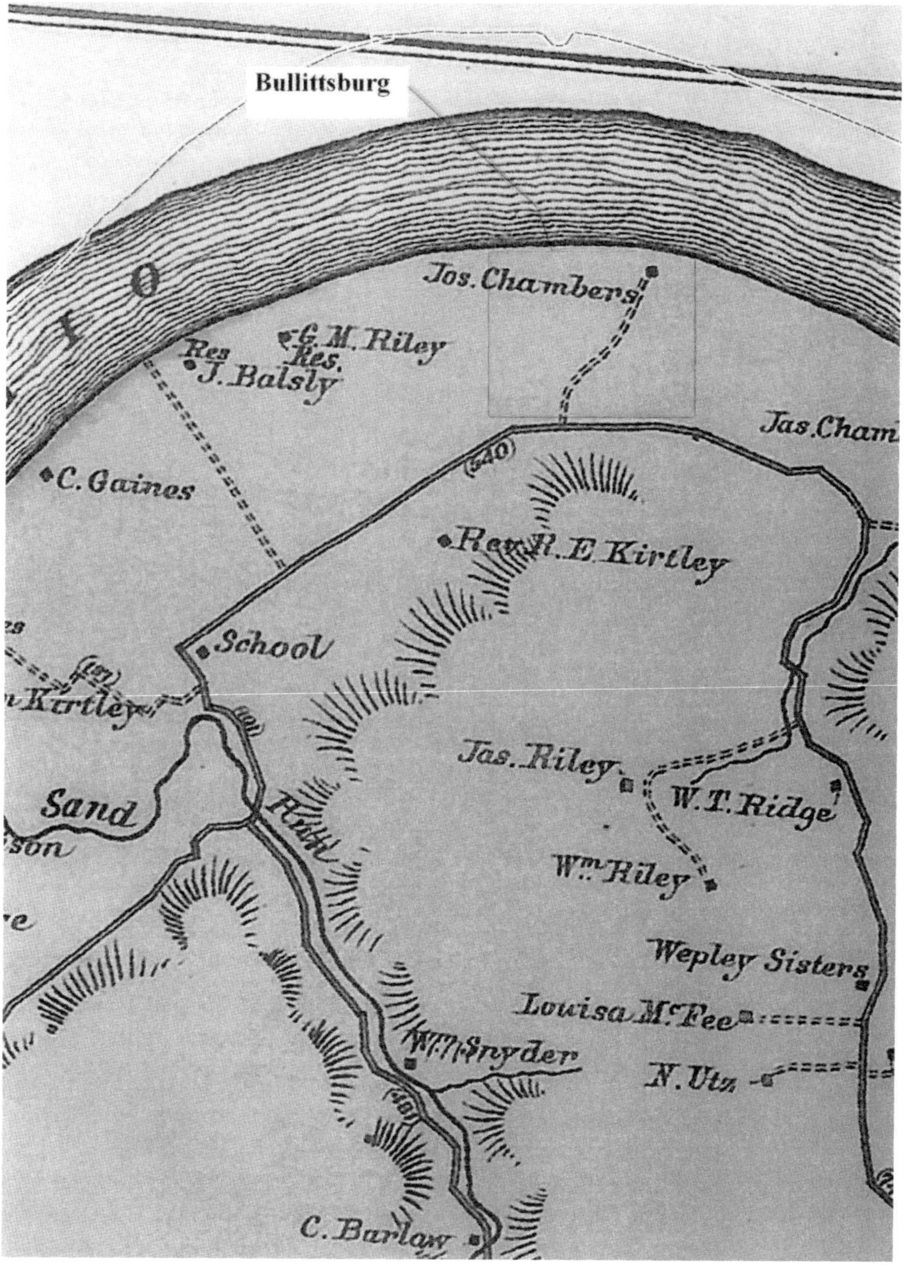


Using the *1883 Atlas of Boone, Kenton and Campbell Counties* map, an approximate location of Bullittsburgh (Bullittsburg) is marked using a description given by W.O. Kirtley for the *Boone County Recorder* in 1905. *Courtesy of the Boone County GIS Database, Boone County Public Library.*

# 3
# Touseytown

About 1804, brothers Zerah, Thomas and Moses Tousey settled on the Ohio River just north of Petersburg at the mouth of Second Creek. The Tousey family lived in Durham, New York, before making the arduous trip to Kentucky. Thomas and Moses quickly established themselves as savvy businessmen, building a mill and a tobacco warehouse and running the ferry across the river to Lawrenceburg.

Though it was never officially a town, the settlement became known as Touseytown. Located between the mouth of Taylor and Second Creeks, the tiny hamlet thrived as the brothers built their businesses, and their growing families settled into their new lives. After the deaths of Moses in 1834 and Thomas in 1839, coupled with the growth of nearby Petersburg and Lawrenceburg, the community faded away. Most of the Tousey children either died young or moved on, leaving the Tousey legacy to die out much like the old town.

When the Touseys made their journey to Kentucky, they brought another family with them. Sometimes family names fade away over time, and the Percival family is one such name. Moses and Thomas married cousins (interestingly, both named Lydia Percival) and brought some of the family with them to settle. Most of the surviving Percival and Tousey children later intermarried with other prominent Boone County families, like Johnson (Cave), Bush and Gaines.

Moses's daughter, Miranda, married Captain Thomas Porter (the Porters were the parents of Albert Gallatin Porter, governor of Indiana, 1881–85), who took over the ferry in 1835. Porter then sold the ferry to the Piatt family, whose land was on the hill above Touseytown. Not much is known about the oldest brother, Zerah (died 1831), though he was the father of Erastus Tousey, whose Federal-style mansion in Burlington still stands (now the Tousey House Restaurant).

Today, all that is left is the cemetery on the hill overlooking the Ohio River. Full of weeds and broken headstones, the final resting place of the Tousey, Percival and Piatt families of Touseytown lies forgotten. The roads that once led to Touseytown—Lawrenceburg Ferry Road and Second Creek Road—now end in an overgrowth of weeds and trees that shows no sign of ever having been home to a thriving community.

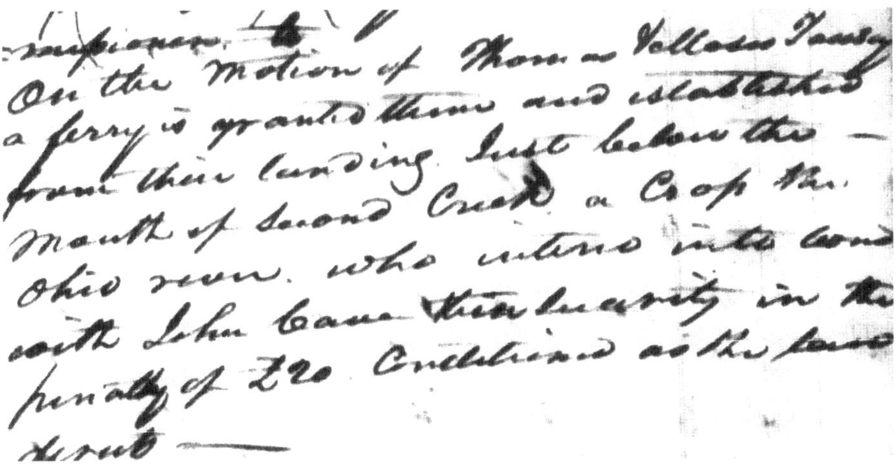

inspection. On the motion of Thomas Tousey a ferry is granted them and established from their landing just below the mouth of Second Creek across the Ohio river. who entered into bond with John Cave their security in the penalty of £20 conditioned as the law directs —

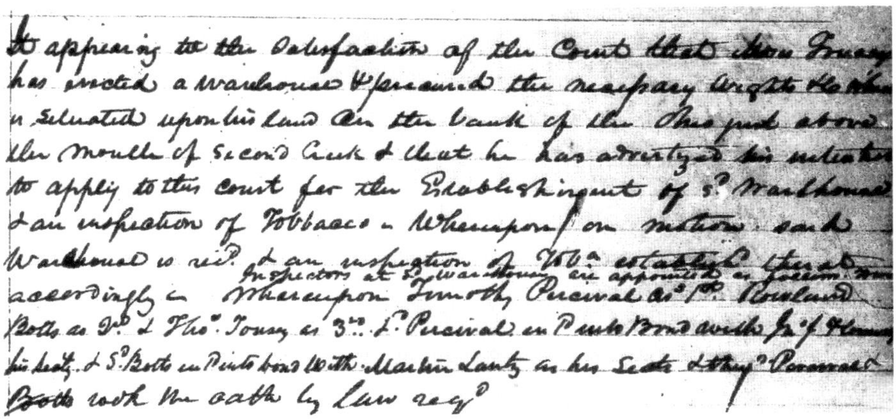

It appearing to the satisfaction of the Court that Thos Tousey has erected a Warehouse & procured the necessary weights &c which is situated upon his land on the bank of the Ohio just above the mouth of Second Creek & that he has advertized his intention to apply to this court for the Establishment of sd Warehouse & an inspection of Tobacco — Whereupon on motion said Warehouse is recd & an inspection of Tobo established thereat accordingly — Inspectors at sd Warehouse are appointed as follows: Whereupon Timothy Percival as 1st Rowland Botts as 2d & Thos Tousey as 3d. T. Percival in Penal Bond with Jno Fleming his secty & sd Botts in Penal bond with Martin Lantz as his Secty & they Percival & Botts took the oath by law reqd

*Above*: A postcard of the summer home of George Bessler at the Lawrenceburg Ferry near Petersburg. The Bessler family emigrated from Germany and lived throughout the Ohio River Valley. *Courtesy of Emmett Witham.*

*Opposite Top*: In 1826, the Boone County Court granted brothers Thomas and Moses Tousey the right to establish a ferry at the mouth of Second Creek (across from Lawrenceburg, Indiana). *Boone County Court Orders. Courtesy of Boone County Public Library.*

*Opposite Bottom*: The court order approving the Tousey Warehouse at Second Creek. The Touseys operated the warehouse, a mill and a ferry during the early nineteenth century. The small community that grew up around the brothers' businesses became known as Touseytown. *Boone County Court Orders 1826. Courtesy of Boone County Public Library.*

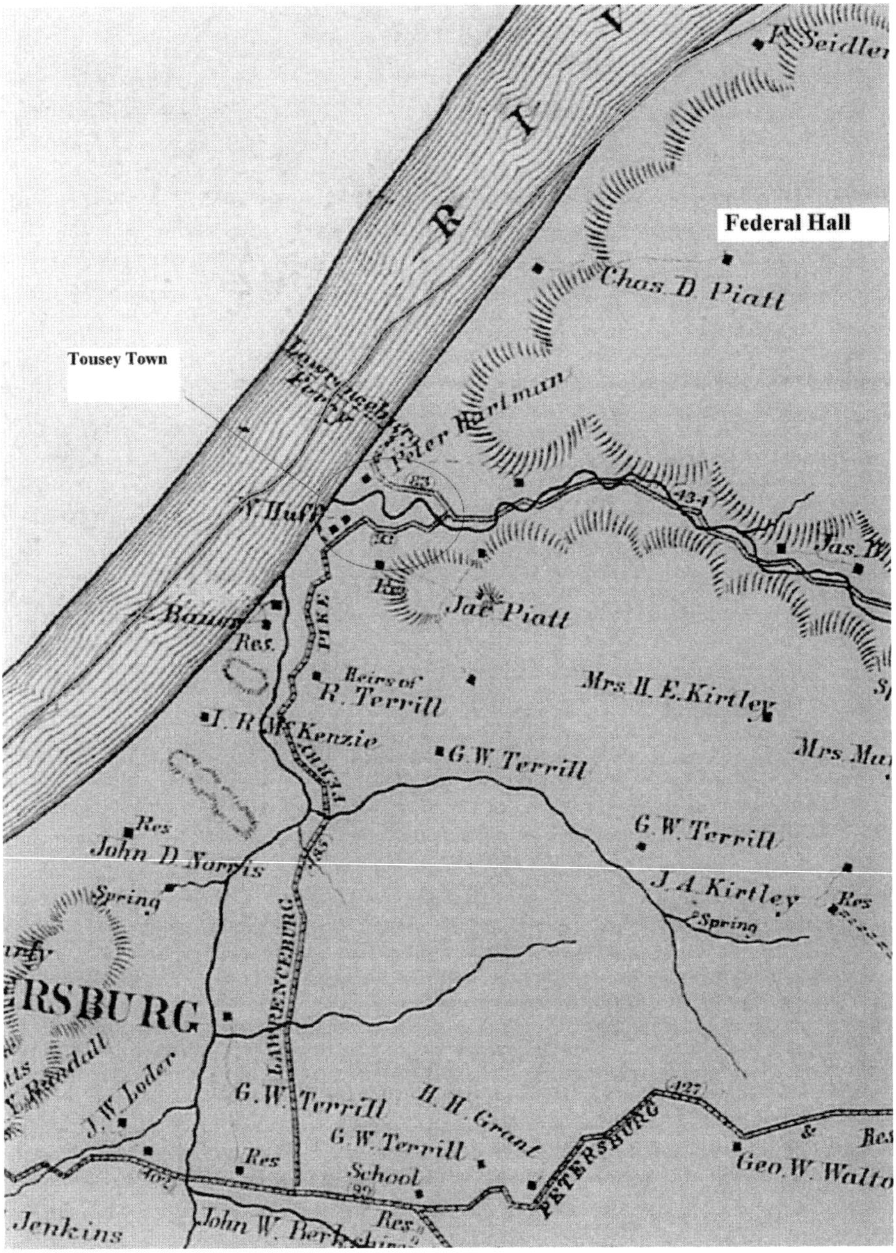


This map from the *1883 Atlas of Boone, Kenton and Campbell Counties* illustrates the location of both Touseytown and Colonel Jacob Piatt's Federal Hall. There is no physical evidence that a town ever stood here, but written accounts of its location, and the location of the ferry, point to the strip of land between Second and Taylor Creeks. Federal Hall stood on the hilltop overlooking Touseytown and the river. *Courtesy of the Boone County GIS Database, Boone County Public Library.*

The Tousey/Piatt cemetery sits on the hill above the old Lawrenceburg Ferry Road. Located on private property, it is now a tangle of brush and broken headstones. *Photograph by Melinda Sartwell.*

## Lawrenceburg Ferry

Lawrenceburg, Indiana, was a gateway for river travel to the west. Many Boone Countians ferried over to Lawrenceburg in order to travel downriver to Louisville, St. Louis and farther destinations. In 1800, John Watts and Jacob Piatt established a ferry operation near Petersburg to accommodate the Lawrenceburg traffic. In 1807, Moses Tousey applied for a ferry license between Touseytown and Lawrenceburg. After Tousey's death in 1834, family members ran the business until 1842, when it was sold to the Piatt family, who owned it for several years. During the nineteenth century, the Lawrenceburg Ferry developed a reputation of being cursed or haunted. The operation changed owners several times due to murder, accidental death and financial ruin. "The Haunted Ferry," written in 1910 by David A. Piatt, a descendent of Jacob Piatt, details the "evil fate" of the various ferry owners. By World War II, it was struggling to survive. The *Pearl of Louisville* was the last ferryboat, running from 1927 to 1945.

The *Carolyn* on the Lawrenceburg, Indiana, side of the Ohio River. The ferry road can be seen on the Kentucky shore. *Courtesy of Don Prout, www.cincinnativiews.net.*

A postcard view of the old Lawrenceburg Ferry on the Indiana shore. *Courtesy of Don Prout, www.cincinnativiews.net.*

This drawing by Cyril Holloway from the article "The Haunted Ferry" by David Piatt depicts a boat accident at the Lawrenceburg Ferry. The ferry was known to have experienced many deaths and accidents over the years. Piatt's article can be accessed in its entirety on Boone County Public Library's website. *Courtesy of Boone County Public Library.*

*Left*: Charles Witham, circa 1920. Witham was born in Belleview and lived in Cincinnati, Ohio, before he was sent overseas during World War I. In the 1930s, he operated the Lawrenceburg Ferry. *Courtesy of Emmett Witham.*

*Below*: The *Pearl of Louisville* at the Lawrenceburg Ferry, circa 1940. *Courtesy of Emmett Witham.*

# Colonel Jacob Piatt

Jacob Piatt was an officer with the First New Jersey Regiment during the Revolutionary War, where he served on General George Washington's staff. According to his journalist grandson, Donn Piatt, Jacob Piatt was seriously injured in the Battle of Monmouth. One of the original members of the Society of the Cincinnati, he used his military land grant to settle in Kentucky, downstream from Cincinnati. Arriving about 1795, Piatt and his wife, Hannah Cooke McCullough, settled on a parcel of land overlooking the Ohio River west of North Bend and built a stately Federal-style mansion. Positioned on a hilltop, Federal Hall had a breathtaking view of the river and landscape. Along with his neighbors, John Brown and Cave Johnson, Piatt was active in local government and was instrumental in the development of Boone County, where he served as county judge for thirteen years.

After Hannah died in 1818, Piatt married Martha Perry in Cincinnati the following year. Colonel Piatt died in 1834 and was buried on the hillside at Federal Hall. Today, the mansion stands in ruins after a fire during the twentieth century. The Jacob Piatt Cemetery still exists but is not actively maintained.

Colonel Jacob Piatt arrived in Kentucky in the late eighteenth century, settling on the hillside above Second Creek overlooking the Ohio River. Here he built an imposing Federal-style mansion aptly named Federal Hall. This aerial view was taken sometime in the 1970s; the old house has since burned. *Courtesy of the Tom Schiffer Collection, Boone County Public Library.*

# 4
# Petersburg

In 1789, Reverend John Tanner moved his family from North Carolina, establishing Tanner's Station, considered the first permanent Euro-American settlement in the area. The site Reverend Tanner chose for settlement was on what was later discovered to be a Fort Ancient Indian village dating to about AD 1200. Fort Ancient Indian villages can be found throughout the Ohio Valley, but the Petersburg site is one of the largest and most studied.

Soon after arriving at Tanner's Station, Tanner's nine-year-old son, also named John, was captured during a Shawnee raid. Shawnee raids were common along the river, and it is said that the boy had wandered away from the cabin when he was taken. The young John Tanner eventually was given to an Ottawa woman and subsequently spent thirty years with the tribes of Canada and Michigan. A book about his experiences was published by Edwin James in 1830. John "the Falcon" Tanner visited Petersburg once in later years, and resident Allan Morgan accompanied Tanner on some of his travels throughout Ohio, Indiana and Michigan. Tanner died under mysterious circumstances in Michigan in 1846.

Reverend Tanner left Kentucky for Missouri before 1800. In 1806, John Grant, a nephew of Daniel Boone, bought 750 acres on the river, seeking to lay out a permanent settlement. Grant quickly established a ferry and, later that year, requested permission from the Boone County Court to lay out the town of Caledonia. Before Caledonia could be established, Grant ran out of money and transferred his land to his son-in-law, John J. Flournoy. Flournoy platted a town on the same site, establishing Petersburg in 1818.

Its location on a high bank of the Ohio River protected the town from flooding but provided easy access for steamboats to dock while loading and unloading cargo. Petersburg developed rapidly when a distillery was established in the 1830s, partnering with the flour mill already in existence. By 1850, Petersburg had the largest population in Boone County. According to the *1883 Atlas of Boone, Kenton and Campbell Counties*, the town boasted the distillery/mill complex, the Boone County Roller Mills, two taverns and other thriving businesses.

Petersburg's prosperity began to wane with the shift of transportation routes following the Civil War. The town was dealt a critical economic blow when the distillery was shut down in the beginning of the twentieth century. The population has continued to decline, and the town has not recovered its earlier commercial success.

A view of Tanner Street looking west, circa 1900. As one of the main streets in Petersburg, the corner just behind the children housed a general store and post office. The Petersburg Christian Church is on the left; at the west end, the hills of Indiana can be seen. *Courtesy of the Petersburg Album Collection, Boone County Public Library.*

Looking into Petersburg from the hill on Route 20, circa 1900. The distillery buildings can be seen at the left and center of the photograph. *Courtesy of the Petersburg Album Collection, Boone County Public Library.*

A view of Market Street in Petersburg, circa 1900. Gordon's Hall can be seen in the distance. *Courtesy of the Petersburg Album Collection, Boone County Public Library.*

A view of First Street near Tanner Street in Petersburg, circa 1900. The Farmer's Bank is in the foreground on the left. *Courtesy of the Petersburg Album Collection, Boone County Public Library.*

The Crisler Hotel was located on the corner of First and Tanner Streets in Petersburg, circa 1900. The building was similar to other houses built in Petersburg's "housing boom" of 1886. Benjamin Crisler and his wife, Laura (née Aylor), ran the hotel from before 1900 until 1920. *Courtesy of the Petersburg Album Collection, Boone County Public Library.*

*Above*: The Carlton House, built about 1825, has been used at various times as a hotel, tavern and private residence. A convenient location on Market Street between Water and First Streets was vital to the enduring success of the hotel and tavern. It is also known as Schramm's Tavern, named for John Schramm, owner during the mid-nineteenth century. *Courtesy of the Petersburg Album Collection, Boone County Public Library.*

*Right*: Charles Schramm partnered with Frank Grant to operate a store in Gainesville (Idlewild) during the 1880s, selling groceries and dry goods. Schramm was the son of John and Catharine Schramm, who operated Schramm's Tavern in Petersburg during the mid-nineteenth century. *Courtesy of the Petersburg Album Collection, Boone County Public Library.*

A view of Petersburg; the old cannery is the long building on the right. *Courtesy of the Petersburg Album Collection, Boone County Public Library.*

The Boone County Roller Mills in Petersburg. The flour mill stood on the riverbank at the corner of Water and Grant Streets. *Courtesy of the Petersburg Album Collection, Boone County Public Library.*

Front view of the Boone County Roller Mills, circa 1900. *Courtesy of the Petersburg Album Collection, Boone County Public Library.*

Interior view of the Boone County Roller Mills. *Courtesy of the Petersburg Album Collection, Boone County Public Library.*

*Left*: The Berkshire family. *Left to right, front to back*: John B. Berkshire, Elizabeth Ryle Berkshire, Frank Walton Berkshire, Maude Berkshire Roseboom, Jean Berkshire Fisher, Mrs. Susan Ryle, unidentified, Frank Belfield Berkshire and William Terrell Berkshire. John B., Maude, Frank B. and William T. were the children of John W. and Fannie (née Walton) Berkshire. *Courtesy of the Petersburg Album Collection, Boone County Public Library.*

*Below*: Youth baseball team in Petersburg, circa 1930. *Courtesy of the Petersburg Album Collection, Boone County Public Library.*

Petersburg baseball team, circa 1920. Community baseball teams flourished in Boone County from the 1870s until World War II. Most towns in the county fielded their own teams, providing entertainment and a friendly rivalry between communities. *Courtesy of the Petersburg Album Collection, Boone County Public Library.*

Unidentified schoolchildren from Petersburg School pose for the camera, circa 1920. *Courtesy of the Petersburg Album Collection, Boone County Public Library.*

*Above*: A group of young people try their hand at fishing off the Petersburg riverbank, circa 1910. *Courtesy of the Petersburg Album Collection, Boone County Public Library.*

*Left*: Julia Loder purchased a large house facing the Ohio River on Front Street in 1857. She and her husband, Lewis A. Loder, ran a hotel and tavern from the home for many years. Mr. Loder was a local magistrate who kept a daily journal from 1857 until 1904. The journal has provided a great deal of information and insight into the daily life of nineteenth-century Boone County residents. *Courtesy of the Petersburg Album Collection, Boone County Public Library.*

*Right*: Sophia Lloyd was the mother of famed pharmacist and author John Uri Lloyd. The Lloyds lived in Petersburg during John Uri's childhood. *Courtesy of the Petersburg Album Collection, Boone County Public Library*.

*Below*: The Witham family poses for a photograph outside their home in Petersburg, circa 1910. Charles Witham (upper right) later owned the Lawrenceburg Ferry, and William Witham (center) served with the Twenty-eighth Regiment of the Pennsylvania Volunteers and fought in the Battle of Gettysburg during the Civil War. *Courtesy of Emmett Witham*.

Blackberry pickers in Petersburg, circa 1910. Berries were popular in making preserves and pies. *Courtesy of the Petersburg Album Collection, Boone County Public Library.*

A view of the Petersburg riverbank, circa 1900. The Loder house can be seen on the left facing the river. Petersburg's topography spared it from the flooding that plagued neighboring communities throughout the years. *Courtesy of the Petersburg Album Collection, Boone County Public Library.*

Located just south of Petersburg, the Aurora Ferry shared transport duties with nearby Horsley's Ferry and the Lawrenceburg Ferry north of town, providing an important link between Kentucky and Indiana. *Courtesy of the Petersburg Album Collection, Boone County Public Library.*

W.R. Moody was a wharfmaster and owned lots in Belleview in 1883. Shown is one of his boats docked by the riverbank in Petersburg. *Courtesy of the Petersburg Album Collection, Boone County Public Library.*

The *Etta Belle* loading passengers in Petersburg, circa 1910. *Courtesy of the Petersburg Album Collection, Boone County Public Library.*

The *Everett Lee* making the trip from Petersburg to Aurora, Indiana. The boat ran from 1945 to 1958. *Courtesy of the Petersburg Album Collection, Boone County Public Library.*

The ferry at Petersburg, circa 1950. *Courtesy of the Petersburg Album Collection, Boone County Public Library.*

A common sight in the nineteenth century, the *Ben Franklin* was one of the many packet boats that ran the Louisville and Cincinnati mail trade. In 1878, it was attempting to dock at the Lawrenceburg wharf near Petersburg when it collided with the wharf boat and sank it. The mail packet survived the accident but was put out of commission three years later. *Courtesy of UW–LaCrosse Historic Steamboat Photograph Collection, University of Wisconsin–LaCrosse, Murphy Library, Special Collections.*

A steamboat and barge on the Ohio River near Petersburg. *Courtesy of the Petersburg Album Collection, Boone County Public Library.*

The *Carolyn* ferries a group to Split Rock, just south of Petersburg, circa 1900. Located at the mouth of Woolper Creek, this once popular destination for outdoor excursions is now a nature conservancy. *Courtesy of the Petersburg Album Collection, Boone County Public Library.*

## PETERSBURG DISTILLERY

In 1816, John J. Flournoy established the Petersburg Steam Mill Company. The flour mill operated independently until 1833, when William Snyder and his brother, John, bought the business and added a distillery. Through the mid-nineteenth century, the distillery became an economic powerhouse in the region. Many Boone County farmers grew corn specifically to sell to the distillery. Distillery workers often lived across the river in Indiana, commuting to work on the Lawrenceburg and Aurora Ferries. By 1860, the business was producing over one million gallons of whiskey.

By the fall of 1861, William Snyder fell into financial trouble and was unable to repay loans he had received to develop the business. According to family tradition, his financial woes were caused by a fraudulent accountant. His property was sold, and Snyder and his family soon left Petersburg for Chattanooga, Tennessee, where a second family-owned distillery was in operation at the time. His son-in-law, Colonel William Appleton, took over the Petersburg Distillery, but the difficult years of the Civil War and high liquor excise taxes forced him to sell a 50 percent interest in the distillery to local farmer Joseph C. Jenkins in 1864. A 25 percent interest was also sold to James Gaff, a partner in T&JW Gaff & Co. Distillery across the river in Aurora, Indiana.

Ownership soon changed again when Jenkins sold his share to Julius Freiberg and Levi J. Workum of Cincinnati in 1869. Gaff and Appleton sold their shares to Freiberg and Workum in 1874. Under Freiberg and Workum, the distillery's production rebounded to pre–Civil War numbers. The distillery soon developed into the largest distillery in the state, once again producing nearly one million gallons of whiskey by 1880. By 1897, the distillery had widened its market to the national and international stages and was able to produce four million gallons of whiskey per year.

Fortunes changed for the Petersburg Distillery in 1899, when Freiberg and Workum sold out to the Kentucky Distilleries and Warehouse Company. The company bought numerous distilleries throughout the state and then promptly started closing them, with Petersburg luckily surviving until 1910 before it was shut down. Even though it was closed, the distillery continued selling its large reserve of whiskey out of the warehouses until late 1918. Most of the buildings were eventually dismantled, though the cooperage and superintendent's house remain.

William and Sarah Snyder, circa 1850s. Snyder developed the Petersburg Distillery and the flour mill into a profitable operation, shipping goods up and down the Ohio River. He sold the complex to his son-in-law in the 1860s after he ran into financial trouble. *Courtesy of the Petersburg Album Collection, Boone County Public Library.*

William T. Snyder. The son of William and Sarah Snyder, William worked in his father's distillery, staying on as a clerk after it was sold. *Courtesy of the Petersburg Album Collection, Boone County Public Library.*

*Left*: Joseph C. Jenkins, a prominent farmer and businessman, was part owner of the Petersburg Distillery in the nineteenth century before it was sold to the Freiberg & Workum Co. *Courtesy of the Petersburg Album Collection, Boone County Public Library.*

*Below*: Prospect Farm, owned by Joseph C. Jenkins, sits on top of the hill from Route 20 overlooking Petersburg and the Ohio River. Jenkins used his considerable wealth to build this imposing Italianate/Greek Revival–style house, which is currently being restored. *Courtesy of the Petersburg Album Collection, Boone County Public Library.*

The Helms house located on Third Street in Petersburg. Everett Helms was the town barber from about 1900 until his death in 1922. Prospect Farm, built by Joseph C. Jenkins just before the start of the Civil War, can be seen on the hilltop in the background. *Courtesy of the Petersburg Album Collection, Boone County Public Library.*

The Petersburg Distillery was bought by Julius Freiberg and Levi J. Workum in 1874. By 1880, it was the largest distillery in the state. It was sold in 1899 to the Kentucky Distilleries and Warehouse Company. The distillery closed in 1910, but whiskey continued to be sold out of storage until late 1918, the beginning of Prohibition. Most of the buildings were dismantled, and the materials were reused in other community buildings. *Courtesy of the Petersburg Album Collection, Boone County Public Library.*

Workers take a break to pose outside one of the storage buildings at the Boone County Distillery. *Courtesy of the Petersburg Album Collection, Boone County Public Library.*

Two men stand on the frozen Ohio River at the Cincinnati Public Landing in this early twentieth-century photograph. Behind them is the *Levi J. Workum* packet boat, owned by the Petersburg Distillery, stuck in the ice after delivering whiskey from Petersburg. *Courtesy of the UW–LaCrosse Historic Steamboat Photograph Collection, University of Wisconsin–LaCrosse, Murphy Library, Special Collections.*

The *Levi J. Workum* docked at the Cincinnati Public Landing, circa 1900. The "whiskey boat" made regular deliveries to Cincinnati from the distillery downriver in Petersburg. *Courtesy of the UW–LaCrosse Historic Steamboat Photograph Collection, University of Wisconsin–LaCrosse, Murphy Library, Special Collections.*

Petersburg Distillery employees take time away from their work for a group photograph, circa 1900. *Courtesy of the Petersburg Album Collection, Boone County Public Library.*

# 5
# Belleview and McVille

## Belleview

In 1815, as Petersburg was being developed just a few miles north, Colonel Edward Meeks was laying out his own town in the river bottoms. Officially platted as Mount Vernon, the name was formally changed to Grant in 1869. The Grant family owned a large amount of land in the area. The name was changed again in 1883 to Belleview (Bellevue). It has often been referred to as Belleview Bottoms to distinguish it from Bellevue in nearby Campbell County. The town was platted in thirty-eight lots laid out along seven streets parallel to the river. The northern edge of Belleview was bordered by the Burlington and Belleview Pike (Route 18), which used to run directly to the river. What is now Route 18 makes a sharp turn at Fourth Street.

As a busy steamboat town, Belleview supported a bustling economy with a hotel, three general stores, two tobacco warehouses, a blacksmith and a basket factory. The basket factory workers used willows harvested from the riverbank to weave baskets to be sold up and down the river. Farmers were prosperous in the fertile river bottomland, considered some of the best in the county, providing plenty of surpluses to be sold. Silas Dinsmoor, adventurer and Indian agent settled in the neighborhood in the late 1830s and remained there until his death. In the 1880s, the Corbin, Botts, Grant and Rice families were prosperous in the little town.

In addition to the business community, Belleview had one of the earliest consolidated schools in the county and two churches—Belleview Christian Church, founded in 1883, and Belleview Baptist Church, created in 1876 after the nearby Middle Creek Baptist Church, chartered in 1803, was destroyed in a windstorm. The church was rebuilt in Belleview and took the name of its new town.

With its low-lying location in the river bottoms, Belleview was victim to numerous floods over the years. The 1937 flood was especially destructive to the riverfront. As a result of the Locks and Dams System, Front Street is now under water. The town is an active community with an elementary school, a general store and a bank.

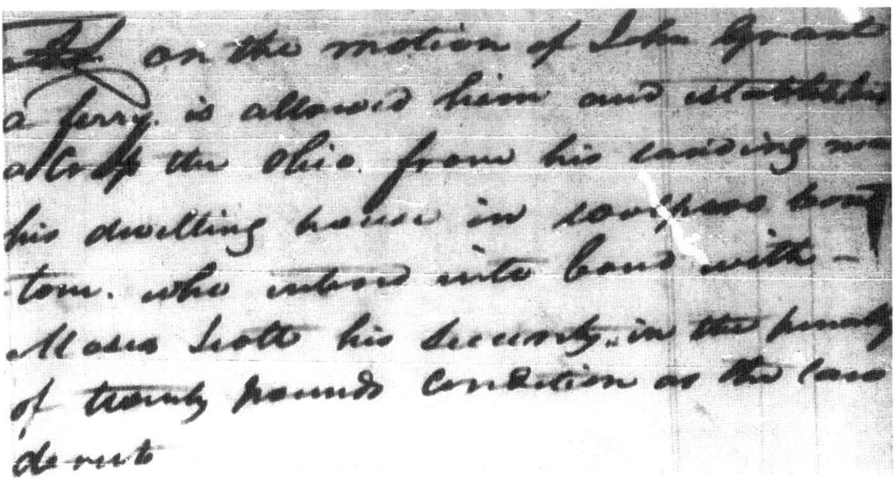

on the motion of John Grant a ferry is allowed him and establish across the Ohio from his landing his dwelling house in town. who entered into bond with Moses Scott his security in the penalty of twenty pounds Condition as the law directs

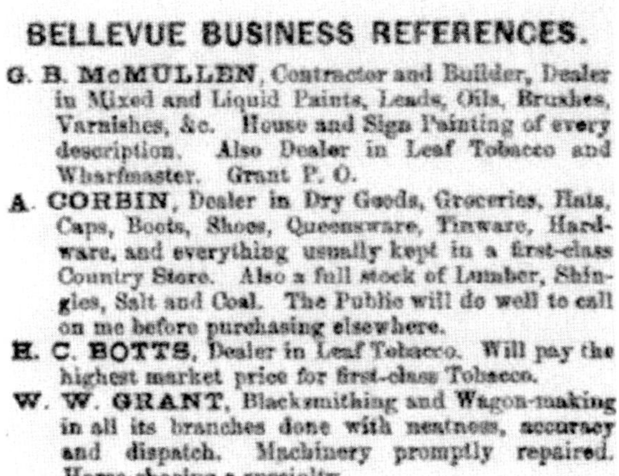

BELLEVUE BUSINESS REFERENCES.

G. B. McMULLEN, Contractor and Builder, Dealer in Mixed and Liquid Paints, Leads, Oils, Brushes, Varnishes, &c. House and Sign Painting of every description. Also Dealer in Leaf Tobacco and Wharfmaster. Grant P. O.

A. CORBIN, Dealer in Dry Goods, Groceries, Hats, Caps, Boots, Shoes, Queensware, Tinware, Hardware, and everything usually kept in a first-class Country Store. Also a full stock of Lumber, Shingles, Salt and Coal. The Public will do well to call on me before purchasing elsewhere.

H. C. BOTTS, Dealer in Leaf Tobacco. Will pay the highest market price for first-class Tobacco.

W. W. GRANT, Blacksmithing and Wagon-making in all its branches done with neatness, accuracy and dispatch. Machinery promptly repaired. Horse-shoeing a specialty.

*Above*: The court order allowing John Grant to establish a ferry on his land in Woolper Bottoms. Later that year, Grant also received permission to lay out a town named Caledonia (later Petersburg). *Boone County Court Orders 1799–1816, July 1806. Courtesy of Boone County Public Library.*

*Left*: In the patron advertisements taken from the *1883 Atlas of Boone, Kenton and Campbell Counties*, Belleview had a thriving business community that faded as railroads and automobiles replaced the riverboat traffic. *Courtesy of Boone County Public Library.*

Belleview (Grant) Christian Church. *Courtesy of Bernie Spencer, www.nkyviews.com.*

The Belleview Store, also known as Hensley's Store, was a center of activity in Belleview for almost seventy-five years, providing goods for residents and serving as a local hangout, as shown in this 1930 photograph. *Courtesy of Boone County Planning Commission.*

An exterior view of the Citizen's Deposit Bank in Belleview. This 1930 photograph shows cashier Charles E. McNeely and assistant cashier John Clore standing in front of the building. A bank has continuously operated in the building since 1927. *Courtesy of the Boone County Planning Commission.*

## LAUGHERY ISLAND

Slightly north of Belleview, a small island sits in the middle of the Ohio River. Laughery Island (also Lochry, or Laughry) was the site of a little-known Revolutionary War battle in 1781 called Lochry's Defeat. Colonel Archibald Lochry and an estimated 110 men he commanded were part of an army raised by George Rogers Clark for a march on the British headquarters in Detroit. The war had spread toward the west as the British recruited Native American tribes to fight against the colonials. A Mohawk leader, Joseph Brant, was part of a British/Indian force that was tracking Clark's army but was too small to attack Clark. After intercepting some messages between Lochry and Clark, Brant waited on the northern shore of the Ohio, past the mouth of the Great Miami River. Hidden from view, Brant waited for Lochry, who decided to stop to rest on the shore near a small island. Brant's force ambushed the colonials, killing Lochry and thirty-six of his men and taking the rest prisoner. Some of the survivors were killed or sent to Native American tribes, but most were sold to the British, who later released them in prisoner exchanges during 1782 and 1783.

The massacre of Lochry's men was a major setback for Clark's campaign, and the march on Detroit was eventually cancelled. After the war, several survivors settled in the region. One survivor, Hugh Steers, settled in Boone County and is buried near Union, Kentucky.

*Lochry's Defeat.* This 1895 drawing depicts the massacre of Colonel Archibald Lochry's battalion in 1781. The island is near present-day Belleview. *From the* Conquest of the Country Northwest of the River Ohio *by William English, vol. 2, drawn by Will Vawter, circa 1895.*

Laughery (Lochry) Island as it looks today. The island is visible when driving down the hill toward Belleview from Rabbit Hash on Route 18. Boat clubs used to go to the island for camping and parties, but it is now privately owned. *Courtesy of the Boone County Planning Commission.*

The new headstone for Hugh Steers at the Steers Cemetery in Union, Kentucky. His original tombstone read: "Hugh Steers, Died Jan 12, 1846, Aged 90 years, Emigrated from Ireland at the age of 18 years, a Revolutionary Soldier." The cemetery has been preserved and is located within the Lassing Pointe Golf Course near the fourteenth hole. *Courtesy of the Boone County Public Library.*

# McVille

The community of McVille, pronounced Mackville, lies next to Belleview in the river bottoms. Laid out by the McMullen brothers in 1881, the small community was only four blocks but had an active steamboat and ferry landing. One of the brothers, Green McMullen, built a home near the river at the corner of Vine and Front Streets. The McMullens had a store and tobacco warehouse nearby. Another brother, Marion, lived a couple blocks away on Scott Street and worked at the warehouse.

Doctor G. Rice and his family owned most of the acreage around McVille in 1883, including the entire riverfront. Rice operated the ferry that was just below the McMullens' warehouse and store. In the 1920s, Rice's Ferry landing was chosen as the location of Lock and Dam No. 38.

The riverfront changed dramatically as construction took the ferry and surrounding shore. The dam was completed in 1926, and at any given time, a dozen or so workers were employed, including a lockmaster. The employees were housed within the town of McVille. The 1937 flood caused extensive damage to the riverbank and surrounding buildings. The McVille Dam remained in place until 1962, when construction of the Markland Dam was completed a few miles south in Gallatin County, Kentucky.

The government buildings on the hill overlooking the dam were left behind after the dam's destruction. In the mid-twentieth century, the site was converted into the Daniel Boone Correctional Institute for Women, which closed in September 1981. In the 1980s, the federal government sold the deteriorated buildings and surrounding property to a private landowner. Since then, the buildings and property have been restored to their 1926 condition, and the buildings have been converted into private rental homes.

Evangeline and Marion McMullen, circa 1890. The McMullen brothers established the town of McVille in 1881. *Courtesy of JoAnn McMullen Suttles.*

Emma McMullen and schoolchildren pose in front of the McVille school. The school was located at the corner of Burlington–Belleview and Waterloo Roads. *Courtesy of the McMullen Collection, Boone County Public Library.*

The building of Lock and Dam No. 38 at McVille in 1925. The Locks and Dams System was established in the early twentieth century to solve the problem of extreme fluctuations of water levels of the Ohio River. *Courtesy of Bernie Spencer, wwwnkyviews.com.*

A barge at Lock and Dam No. 38 in McVille, circa 1950. The dam was in service from 1926 until 1962, when the Markland Dam was built a few miles south in Gallatin County. The Markland Dam replaced the McVille (38), Fernbank (37) and Coney Island (36) dams. *Courtesy of Boone County Public Library.*

A view of Dam No. 38 at McVille looking south toward East Bend. The water line is now just below the trees in the left corner of the photograph. The remains of the walkway down to the dock are still visible. The property is now privately owned and inaccessible to the public. *Courtesy of Boone County Public Library.*

A view of the Lock and Dam No. 38 demolition at McVille in 1963. The site had been in operation for thirty-seven years. In the mid-twentieth century, the site was converted to the Daniel Boone Correctional Institute for Women, which closed in September 1981. *Courtesy of the Boone County Planning Commission.*

The Lock and Dam No. 38 pump house, showing a fourteen-and-a-half-foot low water gage for the Ohio River at the dam. *Courtesy of the Boone County Planning Commission.*

# 6
# East Bend

## Piatt's Landing

Piatt's Landing was located just downstream of Rabbit Hash. According to Piatt family tradition, in 1780 a Canadian trading post was established on the western end of the Upper East Bend Bottoms, where a trapper named DeHart traded in furs. The post was destroyed, and DeHart killed, in 1785, when it was attacked by the Shawnee. This same piece of land was later settled by Robert Piatt in 1808.

Robert Piatt was the nephew of Colonel Jacob Piatt, who built Federal Hall upriver from Petersburg. Robert chose the rich river bottom land of East Bend to establish his farm, where he raised a surplus of crops to sell. Robert was a partner with his cousin, John Piatt (Jacob's son), in the merchant business. They shipped their wares up and down the Ohio River on flatboats. During the War of 1812, Robert and John contracted with the army to supply the troops. Robert was later commissioned a major in the Quartermaster Department.

Returning home after the war, Robert again concentrated on his merchant business. When the steamboats started coming through, he set up a wood yard for the steamers and sold goods to the passengers as they waited for the boats to refuel. As Robert prospered, he built a magnificent riverfront home (later named Winfield Cottage), which was maintained under the guidance of his wife, Nancy, and worked by field hands and house servants.

After Nancy's death, Robert married Moses Tousey's widow, Anne Steadman Tousey. As time passed, Robert started selling parcels of his land to newcomers. Though a commercial district never developed, two churches were founded: East Bend Baptist in 1819 on land provided by Robert Piatt, and East Bend Methodist in 1860. East Bend Methodist, or the "Red Church," no longer holds services, but the building and grounds are maintained by the Rabbit Hash Historical Society.

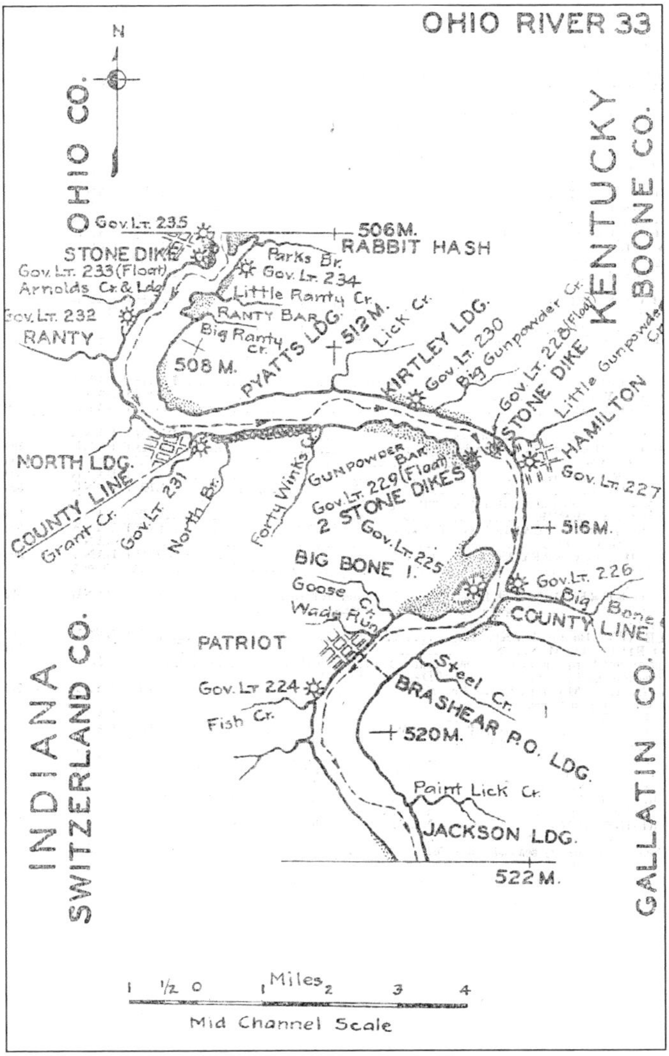


A United States Army Corps of Engineers navigation map of the Ohio River at East Bend. The army was given control of the river in the nineteenth century to deal with the low water levels, sandbars and flooding that caused problems for river traffic. These maps, drawn in 1929, gave boat captains the means to identify difficult navigational areas and technical information needed for safety. *From* The Ohio River: Charts, Drawings, and Description of the Features Affecting Navigation: War Department Rules and Regulations for the River and Its Tributaries: Navigable Depths and Tables of Distances for Tributaries *by United States Army Corps of Engineers, 1929. Courtesy of Boone County Public Library.*

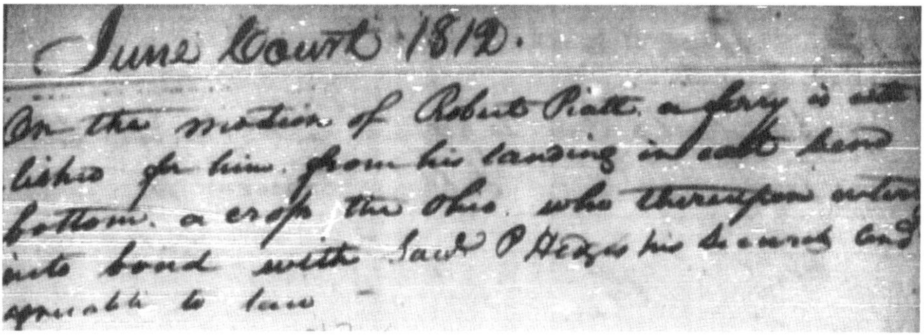

June Court 1812.

On the motion of Robert Piatt a ferry is esta-
blished for him from his landing in East Bend
bottom across the Ohio who thereupon enter'd
into bond with Saml P Hedges his security and
agreeable to law

The court order granting permission for Robert Piatt to establish a ferry. Piatt owned two hundred acres in the East Bend Bottoms, later known as Piatt's Landing, where he established a tobacco warehouse and store. *Boone County Court Orders 1799–1816, May 1812. Courtesy of Boone County Public Library.*

Winnfield Cottage, home of Robert Piatt in East Bend, now the site of a Duke Energy power plant. *Courtesy of the Historic American Buildings Survey, Library of Congress Prints and Photographs Division, Washington, D.C.*

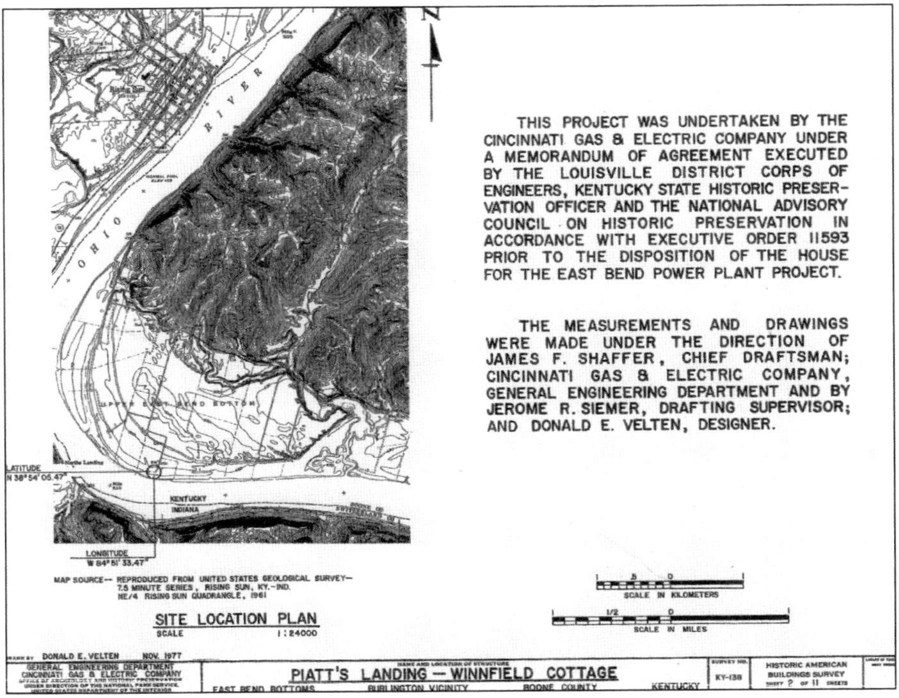


A site location plan drawing for the Cincinnati Gas & Electric plant, now Duke Energy, at Piatt's Landing in East Bend. *Courtesy of the Historic American Buildings Survey, Library of Congress Prints and Photographs Division, Washington, D.C.*

Established in 1860, East Bend Methodist Church was listed on the National Register of Historic Places in 1989. Though it no longer holds services, the building and cemetery are maintained by the East Bend Cemetery Board and Rabbit Hash Historical Society. *Courtesy of the Fitzgerald Collection, Boone County Public Library.*

East Bend Baptist Church was founded in 1819, when it was decided that residents of the bottoms needed their own church. In 1826, Robert Piatt sold a parcel of land to the church trustees in order to build a meetinghouse. The original building stands at the intersection of East Bend and Lower River Roads and currently has an active congregation. *Courtesy of the Fitzgerald Collection, Boone County Public Library.*

An early twentieth-century photograph of the wedding of Bob McNeeley and Jennie Pearl Allen. Mr. McNeeley was pastor at East Bend Baptist Church from 1906 to 1919. Jennie Pearl was part of the prominent Allen family from the Hamilton area. *Courtesy of the Bunger Collection, Boone County Public Library.*

Inez Horton married Jacob Craig after the Civil War. They lived on a shantyboat that they docked along the river from Hamilton up to East Bend. Jacob Craig fought for the Union with the Fifty-fifth Kentucky Volunteer Infantry. *Courtesy of Tony Popp.*

## General Edward Richard Sprigg Canby

One of the new families to settle at Piatt's Landing was the Canby family from Maryland. A member of that family, Dr. Israel T. Canby, married Robert Piatt's daughter Elizabeth in January 1817. Eleven months after they were married, a son was born to the young newlyweds. Edward Richard Sprigg Canby, known as Richard, was a small child when Dr. Canby moved his family to Madison, Indiana, where he established a successful medical practice. While Richard was away at West Point Military Academy, the Depression of 1837 came crashing down on his family. Dr. Canby lost everything and was forced to move back to East Bend, where he depended on the kindness of the Piatt family to survive his financial setbacks.

Richard stayed at West Point, graduating in 1839, and was commissioned in the U.S. Army as a second lieutenant. He served in the Second Seminole War and the Mexican War. In 1861, he was stationed in the New Mexico Territory when the Civil War began and was put in command of the Department of New Mexico. By 1862, he had been promoted to brigadier general. Later reassigned to New York, Canby spent some time with administrative duties before he was moved back west to the Mississippi division after yet another promotion, this time to major general. Canby accepted E. Kirby Smith's surrender of his Confederate forces west of the Mississippi in 1865.

After the war, Canby ended up in the Pacific Northwest, where the Modoc Indians were causing problems for the settlers. In 1873, he was killed by the Modocs during a peace negotiation at which Canby arrived unarmed. He is buried in Indianapolis.

Civil War general Edward Richard Spriggs Canby of Piatt's Landing, son of Dr. Israel Canby and Elizabeth Piatt Canby. General Canby accepted the surrender of Kirby Smith's Confederate forces west of the Mississippi in 1865. In 1873, Canby was killed by the Modoc tribe in the Pacific Northwest while attempting to negotiate a peace treaty. *Courtesy of the Civil War Photograph Collection 1861–1865, Library of Congress Prints and Photographs Division, Washington, D.C.*

## LANDING

In 1838, a community named Landing was platted at the mouth of Landing Creek, also known as Little Gunpowder Creek. The community was also called Hamilton's Landing, and it is sometimes confused with the town of Hamilton downriver. The plat was drawn with 247 lots along the Ohio River that angled up the creek. Landing may have not actually materialized as a town. The *1883 Atlas of Boone, Kenton and Campbell Counties* shows no buildings at Landing, and the area was farmland owned by J.R. Ryle.

While Landing may have not been a functioning town, the creek provided easy access to the Ohio River. Nearby residents would visit entertainment boats docked on the creek. Because of its centralized location along Beaver Road, the Hamilton School was built in 1930 at the edge of Landing. The school was a fixture in the surrounding community until it was razed in 1990 for a new firehouse. The school's doors were used in the entrance of the firehouse, and a time capsule was placed in the 1930 cornerstone to replace the time capsule removed when the school was torn down. Oddly, a mobile home park now sits at the mouth of the creek on lots similar to the original 1838 town plat of Landing.

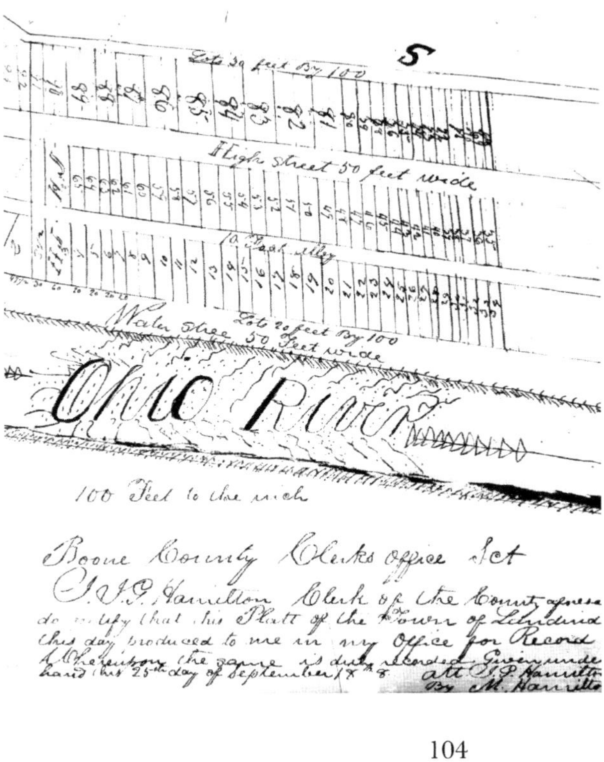


The first page of the plat map for the town of Landing at the mouth of Landing (Little Gunpowder) Creek on the Ohio River. *Courtesy of Boone County Public Library, Boone County Deed Book L.*

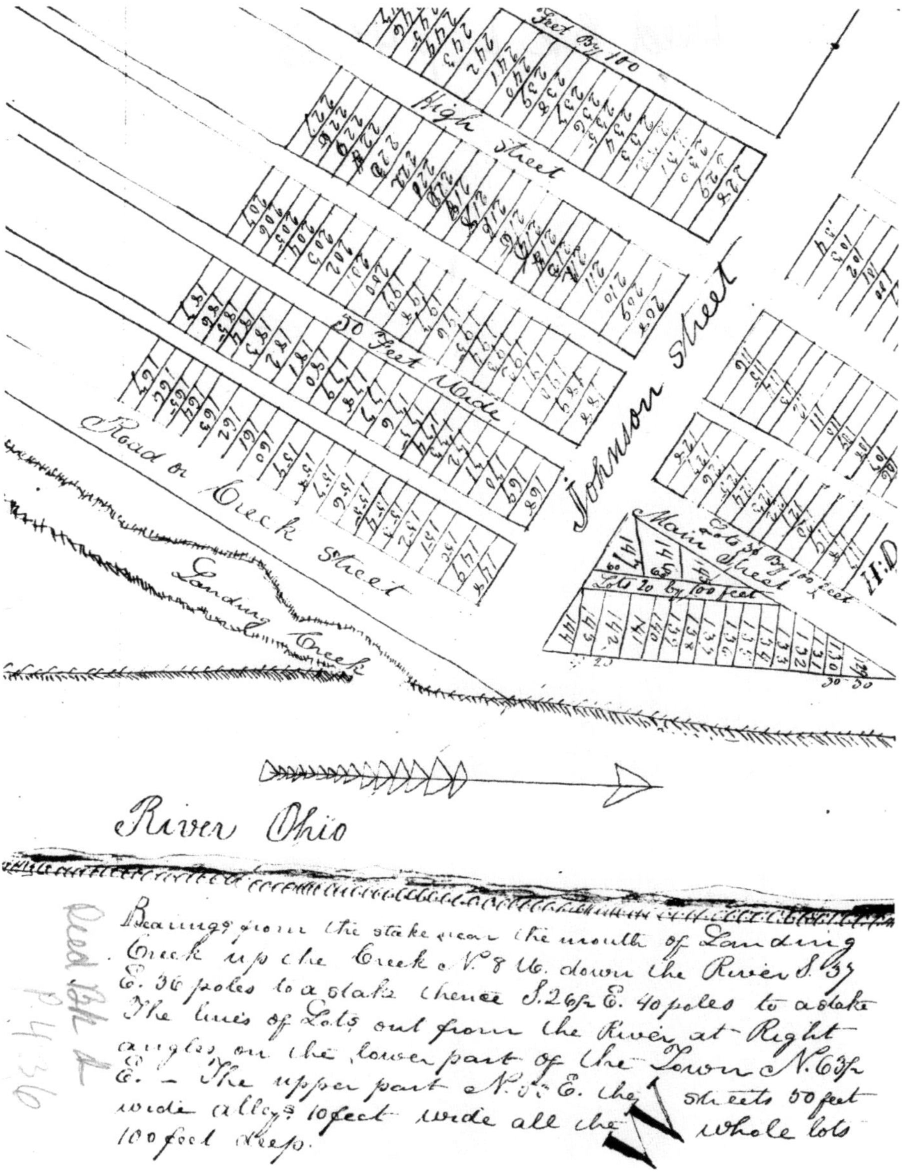


The second page of the Landing plat map. *Courtesy of Boone County Public Library, Boone County Deed Book L.*

The Hamilton School, where Jeanette Smith attended school from 1931 to 1941. The high school classes were discontinued in 1942 due to low enrollment. Located at the entrance to Landing, a firehouse now stands on the property. *Courtesy of Jeanette Edwards Smith.*

Buck Horton, Londa Lee Ryle and J.L. Aylor stand in front of Thomas Huff's general store at Landing, circa 1940. Mrs. Mary Aylor can be seen to the left in the photograph. Thomas Huff was a merchant in the community from as early as 1900. *Courtesy of Jeanette Edwards Smith.*

# Hamilton

Hamilton is the last town along the Ohio River in Boone County. It is located near Big Bone Creek along Ryle Road and was named for one of the early settlers, Joel Hamilton. The town was likely settled in the early nineteenth century due to its proximity to Big Bone Springs and Big Bone Lick. The port was a hub of activity for shipping goods and bringing people in to visit the spring and stay at the Clay Hotel and, in later years, the Big Bone Hotel. Showboats were a popular attraction at the landing, as traveling performers stopped at the various ports on the river to entertain the residents.

Hamilton was a busy town in the nineteenth century, with a mill, two tobacco warehouses, two doctors, a general store, a school and possibly a distillery. In 1883, the Garnett, Johnson, Black, Story and Davis families lived and worked along the river in Hamilton. Dr. John A. Wood advertised a specialization in chronic cases where he practiced at Big Bone Springs. Like the rest of the river towns, diminishing importance of the river took its toll on Hamilton and its neighboring inland communities of Normansville and Big Bone. With the damming of the Ohio River, Hamilton lost riverfront property, where thriving businesses and homes once stood.

This aerial photograph of Big Bone Landing was taken in 2003. Big Bone Landing is a popular destination in modern Boone County. The photo shows Big Bone Creek leading to the Ohio River, visible in the upper left corner. *Courtesy of the Boone County Planning Commission.*

The Allens were an early pioneer family in Boone County, settling in the southern part of the county near Hamilton and Big Bone. *Courtesy of the Bunger Collection, Boone County Public Library.*

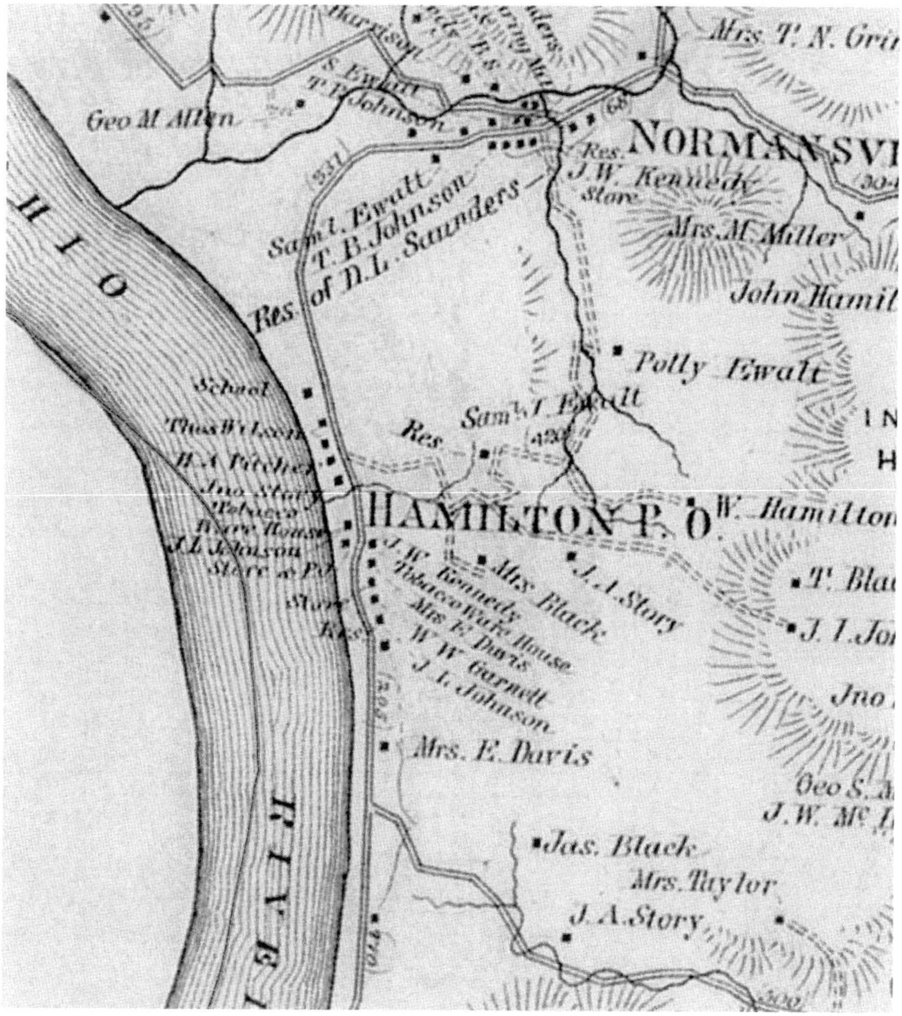


Hamilton, as shown in the *1883 Atlas of Boone, Kenton and Campbell Counties*, grew up along the river just north from the mouth of Big Bone Creek. The town provided the landing for access to Big Bone Lick and its popular salt springs in the nineteenth century. *Courtesy of Boone County GIS Database, Boone County Public Library.*

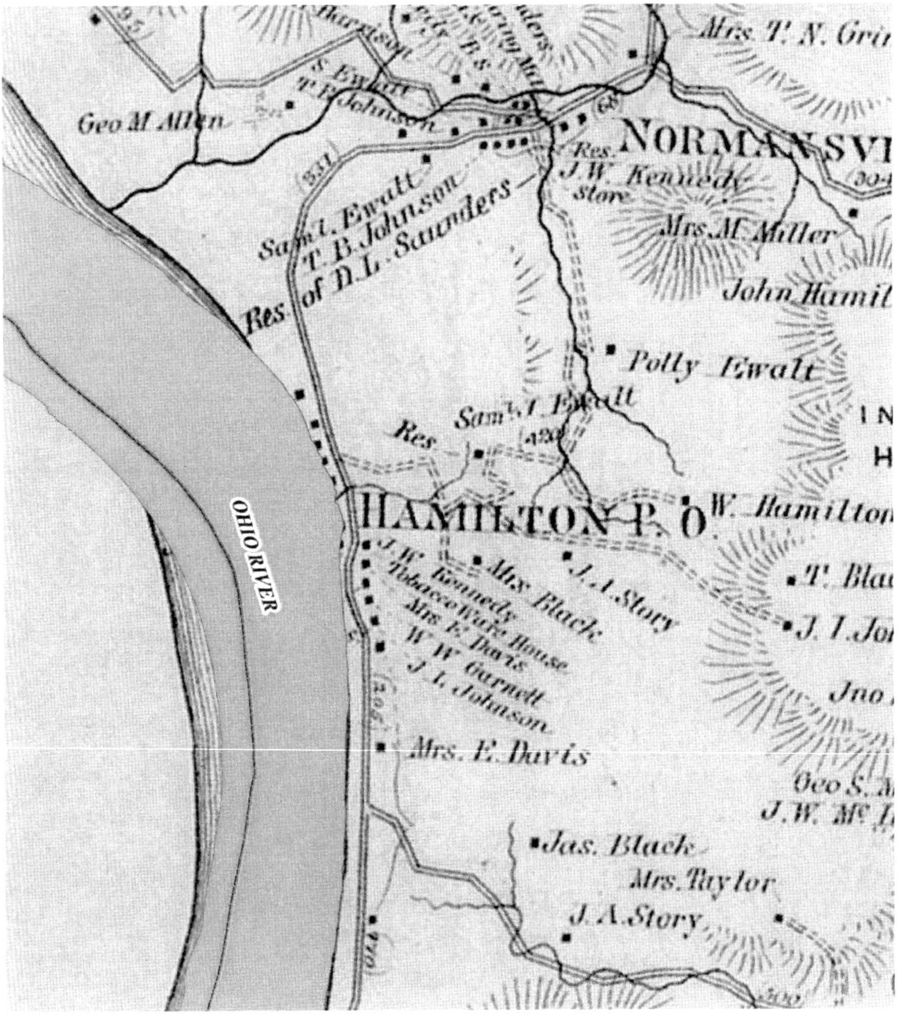


Hamilton with the present-day Ohio River overlay showing that the town lost the entire shoreline west of the road to the river after the dams were built. *Courtesy of Boone County GIS Database, Boone County Public Library.*

A once thriving community, this photo of the old woolen mill from the 1930 *Recorder* shows twentieth-century Hamilton in disrepair. Due in part to its proximity to Big Bone Lick, Hamilton once boasted two tobacco warehouses, two general stores, a post office and a school. *Courtesy of Boone County Public Library,* Boone County Recorder *Historical Edition, September 1930.*

The 1937 flood was a major disaster, submerging entire communities along the river. This photograph shows the water level at Bettie Allen's farm near Route 338, almost one mile inland from Hamilton. *Courtesy of Jeanette Edwards Smith.*

A second view of the flooded Bettie Allen property near Hamilton in 1937. The farm was almost a mile inland at Normansville. Notice the outbuilding roof barely visible above the water line. *Courtesy of Jeanette Edwards Smith.*

Marvin Allen and his mother, Bettie, at the Allen Farm near Hamilton, circa 1920. Bettie was the wife of Benjamin C. Allen. Benjamin died in 1928. *Courtesy of Jeanette Edwards Smith.*

William McSwain (seated in buggy) was a farmer in the Hamilton/Big Bone vicinity in the early twentieth century. He later moved across the river to Patriot, Indiana, where he died in 1938. *Courtesy of the Bunger Collection, Boone County Public Library.*

A peaceful winter landscape shows the beauty of the Kentucky hills in this photograph taken near Hamilton. *Courtesy of Jeanette Edwards Smith.*

The river was not only used for transportation and commercial trade, but it also served a spiritual purpose as a place for baptisms. This photograph of a Big Bone Baptist Church baptism was taken in 1944 near Landing. *Courtesy of Jeanette Edwards Smith.*

An early twentieth-century baptism in the Ohio River near Landing, involving parishioners from nearby Big Bone Baptist Church. *Courtesy of Jeanette Edwards Smith.*

## Big Bone Island

Big Bone Island was a small natural deposit of sand and gravel just below the mouth of Big Bone Creek. The island was never inhabited. However, the flat, partially wooded terrain made it a popular camping and fishing spot up through the twentieth century. Years of river ice and rising water levels slowly eroded the sandy island. During the winter of 1977, the Ohio River was ice packed, and by spring, the island was completely gone.

The island's location, straddling the Boone and Gallatin county line, led to some good-natured controversy about which county actually owned the island. By 1970, changing water levels and shifting deposits had reshaped the island, leaving it entirely within the borders of Gallatin County. This prompted Boone County judge executive Bruce Ferguson to launch an "invasion" to take back the island. In the summer of 1973, as part of the celebrations to commemorate the 175th anniversary of Boone County, Judge Ferguson led a two-pronged attack to reclaim the island.

"The Boone Volunteer Defenders" stormed the beachhead and secured the provisions for the mission: the beer keg. Once in position, the invaders trained the cannon at the potential enemy forces: Gallatin County. Judge Ferguson soon arrived, his father's captured samurai sword lifted high, declaring victory. Celebrations were cut short when air support finally arrived and the pilot mistook the celebrants as enemy combatants. Observing strict radio silence, the pilot launched the prepared flour bombs at the unsuspecting revelers. Believing it to be an enemy counteroffensive, the artillerymen returned fire. Fortunately, there were no casualties from this incident of friendly fire.

The *C.T. Dumont* packet boat, built in Cincinnati in 1864, crashed at Big Bone Island in December 1865. Shortly after rebuilding, the boat was hit by a tornado near Warsaw, Kentucky. Rebuilt for a second time, the *Dumont* then ran the Cincinnati–Louisville line. The *Dumont*'s main claim to fame is that it was the transport for General Ulysses S. Grant and his family from North Bend to Cincinnati. *Courtesy of Bernie Spencer, www.nkyviews.com.*

Asa Rouse (left), Barbara Brakefield and John Brakefield enjoy a camping trip on Big Bone Island in 1947. A popular boating and camping destination, the island has completely disappeared, claimed by erosion and the rising waters of the Ohio River. *Courtesy of Boone County Public Library.*

Boone County judge executive Bruce Ferguson led the invasion to recapture Big Bone Island in the summer of 1973. Due to shifting sand and gravel deposits, the island had "drifted" downriver past the Boone/Gallatin county line by 1970. In the photo, the airplane was dropping flour bombs on the ground troops in an unfortunate friendly-fire incident. *Courtesy of Randy Cochran.*

# Conclusion

The communities described in the preceding pages were shaped both literally and figuratively by the Ohio River. The river provided the most efficient transportation for both goods and people, and settlements developed to support and take advantage of this transportation network. Once river commerce declined, due to railroads and improved overland roads, the prosperity of most of these communities went with it. The damage was further exacerbated by the damming of the Ohio River. Entire sections of towns like Taylorsport and Belleview now lie under the muddy Ohio waters.

For most of the last fifty years, development in Boone County was centered along and near the interstate corridor. Now as development begins to encroach on these once forgotten communities, it is important to reflect and remember those who came before us. This book is an attempt to acknowledge and honor the people who helped shape this county and region.

# Bibliography


Becher, Matthew E. *The Distillery at Petersburg, Kentucky: Snyder's Old Rye Whiskey*. Burlington, KY: Boone County Planning Commission, 2002.

Boone County Public Library Local History and Genealogy. "Chronicles of Boone County." http://bcpl.org/lhg/cbc/doku.php.

*Boone County Recorder.* "Big Doings at the Celebration of the Fern Bank Dam, Which Begins Next Monday." August 31, 1911.

———. Charles L. Hempfling obituary. February 6, 1969.

———. Historical edition. September 4, 1930.

Bottorff, Katherine Piatt. "The Piatts of East Bend, Boone County Kentucky 1803–1865." http://bottorff.org/Piatt.htm.

*Campbell County Court Order Book*. Alexandria, KY, n.d.

Capek, Michael. *Lively Stones: A Narrative History of Belleview Baptist Church, 1803–2003*. Knoxville, TN: Valley Publishing, 2002.

Carneal, Thomas D., to Robert Piatt. *Boone County Deed Book D*. Burlington, KY, n.d.

*Cincinnati Enquirer*. "Acquisition of Belleview Institute Urged." September 30, 1981.

Coney Island Company to C.O. Hempfling. *Boone County Deed Book 45*. Burlington, KY, n.d.

Farming Oral History Project, 2007–08. *From Teams to Tractors: Farming in Boone County 1940–2008*. Burlington, KY: Boone County Public Library, 2009.

Griffing, B.N. *Atlas of Boone, Kenton and Campbell Counties, Kentucky*. Philadelphia: D.J. Lake, 1883.

Hansel, Mark. "Valley Orchards Returns to Its Roots." nky.cincinnati.com.

Johnson, Cave. "The Early Days of Kentucky: Some Reminiscences from the Life of Col. Cave Johnson, Together with an Obituary Written at the Time of His Death." *Boone County Recorder*, February 1, 1877.

*Kentucky Post*. "Cast in Stone." May 7, 1990.

———. "Fire Station Dedicated." September 9, 1991.

Kirtley, Elizabeth McMullen. *Relationship of the Kirtley Family to the Bullittsburg Baptist Church, 1796–1904*. Burlington, KY, 1994.

Kirtley, Elizabeth McMullen, and Carlene Stephens. *East Bend Baptist Church, 1819–1994: 175 Years Continuous Service at 12246 Lower River Road*. Burlington, KY, 1994.

Kirtley, W.O. "Letter to the Editor." *Boone County Recorder*, January 11, 1905.

McHenry, Chris. *The Best Men of Westmoreland*. Lawrenceburg, IN, 1981.

Piatt, David A. "The Haunted Ferry." *World Wide Magazine* (1910).

Reis, Jim. "Pieces of the Past: Controlling the Ohio's Flow—Before Markland was Lock No. 38 in Boone County." *Kentucky Post*, February 24, 2003.

———. "Pieces of the Past: Taylorsport Is Truly a Survivor Among Towns." *Kentucky Post*, July 10, 2000.

Rose, Theodore Cuyler. *The Tousey Family in America*. Elmira, NY: Osborne Press, 1916.

Schiffer, Thomas D. *Big Bone Island Invasion*. Burlington, KY, 2009.

Spencer, J.H. "Cave Johnson." In *A History of Kentucky Baptists*. Vol. II. Cincinnati, OH: Printed for the author, 1886. Reprint, 1984.

Steitzer, Stephanie. "Land on River Could Be Park." *Kentucky Post*, April 8, 2004.

Tenkotte, Paul A., and James C. Claypool. *The Encyclopedia of Northern Kentucky*. Lexington: University Press of Kentucky, 2009.

U.S. Army Corps of Engineers. "Pittsburgh District—Navigation." http://www.lrp.usace.army.mil/nav/nav.htm.

Warner, Jennifer S. *From Mastodons to the Millennium*. Boone County Bicentennial Committee, 1998.

Wimberg, Robert J. *Amusement Parks of Greater Cincinnati and Northern Kentucky*. Cincinnati: Ohio Book Store, 2002.

Yealey, A.M. *History of Boone County, Kentucky: Reprint of Articles Published in Newspapers Over a Period of Fifty Years*. Covington, KY: William Fitzgerald, 1960.

# About the Contributors

Originally from western New York, BRIDGET B. STRIKER is the local history coordinator at the Boone County Public Library. Bridget has been at the library since 2001 and has led the Local History Department since 2005. Bridget holds a BS in anthropology and a master's degree in library and information sciences. She has served on the Boone County Historic Preservation Review Board since 2004.

DONALD E. CLARE JR. is one of the most recognized personalities in Boone County historic preservation. Don has served on the Boone County Historic Preservation Review Board since its creation in 1986, serving as chairman for ten years. He also is the president of the Rabbit Hash Historical Society, which he established in the 1980s. Over the years, Don has coauthored and contributed to many books and articles regarding Boone County history. In 2010, he was presented with the Ida Lee Willis Memorial Foundation Preservation Service Award from the Kentucky Heritage Council.

JENNIFER GREGORY has been the virtual services librarian for the Boone County Public Library since 2007. She specializes in digitizing Kentucky historic materials for online access. In 2006, Jennifer published a pictorial history of Northern Kentucky University, where she was employed as special collections librarian and university archivist. Jennifer holds a BA in classical humanities and a master's degree in library and information sciences.

C. ADAM HARTKE has been a staff member of the Local History Department at the Boone County Public Library since 2009; he focuses on digital projects. Adam is currently enrolled in Northern Kentucky University's master of arts in public history program. Adam specializes in urban planning and has recently completed a project for the City of Fort Mitchell.

MELINDA SARTWELL is a Northern Kentucky native with a BA in history from Northern Kentucky University, where she is currently working toward her master of arts in public history. Melinda published a pictorial history of Walton and Verona, Kentucky, in 2009. From 2005 to 2009, she worked at the Schlacter Archives in the Steely Library at Northern Kentucky University.

LAURIE WILCOX has been at the Boone County Public Library since 2000 and a staff member of the Local History Department since 2007. Having finished her BA in independent studies in 2007, Laurie has focused on oral history projects both for the library and independently. In addition, Laurie is an experienced genealogist and coordinates genealogy programming for the library.